How To

Strengthen Your Winning Business Personality

By Brenda Smith

The Career Press
62 Beverly Rd., PO Box 34
Hawthorne, NJ 07507
Toll-Free 1-800-CAREER-1

How To Strengthen Your Winning Business Personality, By Brenda Smith. ISBN 0-934829-57-8, $11.95

Copies of this volume may be ordered by mail or phone directly from the publisher. To order by mail, please include price as noted above, $2.50 handling per order, plus $1.00 for each book ordered. Send to: The Career Press Inc., 62 Beverly Rd., PO Box 34, Hawthorne, NJ 07507

Or call Toll-Free 1-800-CAREER-1 to order using your VISA or Mastercard or for further information on all books published or distributed by The Career Press.

Table of Contents

Where Do You Fit?

Chapters

Appendices

Index

Acknowledgements

My Heartfelt Thanks To:

The thousands of clients at AIMS (Aptitude Inventory Measurement Service) in Dallas, Texas. Their reports of successes and failures and stories of career experiences made this book possible.

Pierce B. Watters and AIMS staff members Irvin C. Shambaugh, John W. Gaston, and Deborah Stewart Tatum for sharing their knowledge and expertise over the years.

Ronald W. Fry, for his superb editing of the book.

Lastly, my husband, Rosser J. (Jeff) Smith, III, for much of my first-hand and vicarious exposure to the realities of the business world and for his active encouragement.

One

How This Book Can Make *You* Successful

Mercedes or BMW? Motor Yacht or Sailboat? Castle or Mansion? Corner Office or VP Title?

We all seemingly want different things out of life. At least different *specific* things.

But are our desires really so different? I think all of us—whether we've been in the work-a-day world for decades or are just graduating from school—probably have the same *general* hopes and desires—to be happy, earn money, feel fulfilled, be successful. However differently we each define "success," most of us can at least agree that we want "it!"

Just as probably, too many of us are struggling to deal with a reality that has left us *un*happy, *un*fulfilled, *un*successful...and *un*rich. The tragedy in today's business world is that you are not alone. Stress and burnout are becoming all-too-common accompaniments to our drive for the Great Brass Ring.

What's missing? Why *aren't* you rich and successful?

Congratulations! You *Are* Rich!

I've got a surprise for you. You *are* rich and, by using what you already possess, can *be* successful. You already have something all the money in the world could never buy. You were born with it, or at least created it very early in your life. You cannot count it or spend it at the corner grocery, but you can objectively measure it and invest it. And if you take the time and make the effort to identify and maximize it, it will enable you to generate the tangible riches you desire.

What are these riches? *Aptitudes*—those innate abilities and talents that combine to define the "(wo)man in the mirror"—the characteristics that combine to form your talent, your brain power...in many ways, your whole identity.

Whether or not you know you have them, whether or not you've ever used them, they are inside you, *waiting* to be used. *Regardless* of your level of education or lack of it; *regardless* of your job experience; even *regardless* of your demographic background. And whatever future schooling or work you do will not significantly change them...or the fact that whenever you decide to finally employ them, they will open the door to achieving your potential.

Use 'Em...Or Else!

So what? Why should you want to read a whole book about aptitudes?

For one, these hidden riches actually become *liabilities* if you do not use them. Your aptitudes must be "spent" if you want to avoid the boredom and burn-out that attacks anyone who, even if employed, never finds opportunities to invest his innate abilities.

Not using your aptitudes is like repressing an emotion. Frustration builds and eventually affects not only the way you feel, but also the way you behave. I can make a strong case that the cause of stress or depression in all-too-many people lies in the fact that they *know* they're missing *some*thing; they just don't have a clue what it is.

The bottom line is simple: "Use them...or else."

Because if you do use them—if you concentrate on the things that you do *better* than others, *use* your talents to their greatest potential—your aptitudes are your greatest assets in a business career. You will always have them. They are indestructible. Properly used, they earn "interest," just like any investment, and pay out both financial and emotional dividends.

Aptitudes also directly affect how you interact with other people. After all, *they* have aptitudes, too! Especially in a business career, dealing with bosses, co-workers, and subordinates (not to mention family and friends) is a significant part of daily life. Developing an understanding of your aptitudes will enable you to recognize those of your boss, co-workers, subordinates, clients, etc., knowledge that can dramatically affect your effectiveness on the job.

Despite his position, your boss might actually be weak in some of the talents necessary to do his job. You'll make yourself invaluable to him by identifying his weaknesses and concentrating on the things he finds difficult.

Each of your co-workers will have a different work style. Recognizing this, you'll communicate better with each one by understanding each individual's distinct "pattern of thinking."

Each of your subordinates will be particularly suited to different tasks. You'll delegate more effectively by recognizing each of their strengths and weaknesses.

Each of your clients will perceive things differently. You'll modify your approach to each client, based on what *he* thinks is important.

Aptitudes affect the way a person behaves and the way he thinks about things. Your ability to perceive these factors will spell the difference between effectual communication and complete misunderstanding, between efficiency and chaos, between success and promotion and joining the unemployment line.

Where Do I Start?

Now that I have whetted your appetite and roused your curiosity, what do you do? Start with Appendix III—"Test Your Own Aptitudes." By the time you finish the whole test, you will have made an excellent start to finding out exactly where *you* fit: How do you look at the world? What's your personality "type?" What specific conceptual and performing aptitudes should you be using?

Chapter 2 explains each of these aptitudes in detail and will enable you to understand more about your particular strengths and weaknesses. At end of chapter 2 is a series of charts. Based on the aptitudes you've discovered, you'll be able to identify which of the Aptitude Profiles in this book is most like you—Persuader (Chapter 3), Diplomat (4), Communicator (5), Shirt-Sleeves Manager (6), Gnome (7), Delegator (8), Wheeler-Dealer (9), Entrepreneur (10), Consultant (11) or Small Business Owner (12).

Each of these ten chapters is similarly formatted. The left-hand page opposite the chapter heading summarizes the strong and weak aptitudes of that chapter's Aptitude Profile. Then, using a number of examples of real-life people, the text of each chapter will illustrate that Profile "in action" and help you understand how it differs from the others in this book.

At the end of each chapter, I've included three lists. The first is of the careers particularly right for that specific Profile. Don't expect to find the single "perfect" career or job that exists only for you. As you'll soon see, there are sometimes *hundreds* of business occupations appropriate for each Aptitude Profile. (Where available, I have included the DOT—Dictionary of Occupational Titles—reference number for each job title listed. If you consult this book in your local library, you will find a brief description of each of these jobs.)

There are thousands, if not *tens* of thousands of potential job titles. Understanding who you are simply eliminates the thousands of *bad* choices that may spell career disaster for you. You'll be in a better position to select the opportunity that best fits you.

The second list is of the professional and trade organizations appropriate to that Aptitude Profile. To get further information on these organizations (and others in allied fields), consult The Encyclopedia of Associations, available in most libraries nationwide.

The third list is of business publications appropriate to that Aptitude Profile. Further information on these is also available at your local library. Consult The Directory of Magazines (Oxbridge Communications) or Standard Rate & Data Service. Or ask your librarian if they have back issues of any of the cited publications—many libraries will.

There are two other appendices you will find helpful. Appendix 1 lists every aptitude discussed in this book and summarizes the characteristics associated with each. Use it as a reference guide and refer to it whenever you need to.

Because there is virtually *no* career Entrepreneurs or Small Business Owners cannot realistically consider, there is no list of "appropriate" careers at the end of chapters 10 or 12. Appendix 2, however, lists a wide variety of small businesses appropriate to those of you with particular combinations of aptitudes. If you're thinking of starting your own business, you will find this appendix invaluable.

I Want To Be A Dancer

As you read through this book, you will quickly discover (as the title certainly implies) that it concentrates exclusively on *business-related careers*. The primary reason is that the business world offers more opportunities to more people than any other field.

Unlike many professions, a college degree with a specific major is not essential for success in business. In fact, specific aptitudes often impact your success more dynamically than any combination of majors or courses. Though many larger corporations require a degree, what you study is fast becoming less significant than ever before.

For those with very little formal education, business is one of only a few places where you can still start at the bottom and work your way up the corporate ladder, sometimes to the very top. Business opportunities exist in large cities, small towns, and rural areas. Business offers careers suitable for flamboyant glad-handers, reserved loners, and everyone in between.

The scope of this book and, frankly, length limitations, do not afford me the freedom to address the countless careers outside the world of business. The brain surgeon, criminal lawyer, professional athlete, poet, and high school history teacher are not specifically discussed here.

Yet those of you with such aspirations would still benefit from reading this book and discovering your own Aptitude Profile; all of the aptitudes discussed are just as applicable to virtually *any* profession, business or otherwise.

Enough introduction. You've waited long enough for a roadmap to success. It's time to get started on this exciting journey.

Two

What Your Aptitudes Mean

Before we begin defining each of the aptitudes discussed in this book, let's clarify a few general rules that apply to all of them.

First, *strong aptitudes require outlets.* You will never be really fulfilled if you do not find opportunities in which to invest your talents. If you fail to channel these strengths into productive ventures, you will undoubtedly be frustrated. On the other hand, consciously exercising your talents and abilities will definitely increase your job satisfaction and enhance your chances for career success.

Second, *you can compensate for a weak aptitude.* A weakness is not an excuse for failure. With hard work, you *can* overcome a lack of natural talent. But working to change a weak aptitude is very time consuming. You may decide it's more advantageous to invest the same time and energy in maximizing your *strengths*.

Third, *having a few strong aptitudes can be better than having too many.* You will discover that once you have identified two or three strengths, you will be sufficiently prepared to focus your energies on the career that best meshes with your general Aptitude Profile.

For those of you with four or more strong aptitudes, be careful! *Too many* aptitudes in most business settings spells trouble. You may find that your abundance of ability makes learning a new job easy, but that, once mastered, the exciting becomes routine, boredom attacks, and you begin seeking out new challenges.

Small companies that offer positions in which you can wear a number of "hats" may provide the necessary outlets for those of you with an abundance of aptitudes. You may also consider starting your own company or consulting as alternatives to a "normal job" in the corporate setting. Many Entrepreneurs demonstrate numerous strong aptitudes.

Fourth, *some aptitudes are more important than others.* Your Frame of Reference and Personality Type (see pp. 15—17), for example, govern your interactions with other people. In the business world, where communication is so vital, these characteristics can "make or break" you. Your Conceptualizing Aptitudes (see pp. 17—20) dictate the importance of imagination and problem solving in your work. How aware you are of these specific qualities can significantly impact any career decision and the level of satisfaction you will experience.

Finally, *be aware of your Performing Aptitudes* (see pp. 20—29), which affect how quickly and easily you carry out certain tasks. As you climb the career ladder, these aptitudes may diminish in importance as you delegate the duties that require them. This can be a source of frustration unless you find other outlets, such as hobbies, for these abilities .

The two charts at the end of this chapter (pp. 30—33) will enable you to quickly see which aptitude combinations best mesh with specific business career combinations. By matching your aptitudes to these flow charts, you can pinpoint the Aptitude Profile chapters (3—12) pertinent to you.

Frame of Reference

What is your natural way of looking at things? Do you see things pretty much the way most people do? Or are you always the one with the unique viewpoint? Such tendencies suggest your *Frame of Reference*—whether you are a *Generalist* (the former) or a *Specialist* (the latter).

Generalists are very people oriented—they find it easy to communicate on an informal basis and to cooperate as members of a team. Naturally relating to their peers and co-workers, Generalists interact well in most work situations. A Generalist frame of reference is vital in any business that demands teamwork or constant customer contact.

The biggest problem for any Generalist is concentrating on a very narrowly-defined job—he functions best when he has to know a little bit about a lot of things, not everything about one thing.

If people skills are not your forte and you are the alternate voice in many discussions, then you should avoid work situations that require this team mentality. You are most likely a *Specialist,* "marching to the beat of a different drummer." Every Specialist has his own frame of reference—a "wave length" all his own—which differs even from those of other Specialists.

Specialists achieve success in careers that emphasize individual effort over people skills. Jobs that require constant coordination and compromise with other people are at best difficult, at worst impossible. Many Specialists tell horror stories of their efforts to "fit in."

If you are a Specialist, you will soon discover that capitalizing on your differences is far more productive than ignoring them and trying to be like everybody else, a goal which you will likely not achieve anyway.

Specialists should attempt to develop a particular skill or expertise, which will afford them the independence they thrive on. As they gain this expertise, people will be drawn to their competence *regardless* of their people skills...or lack of them.

Should you still be uncertain about whether you are a Generalist or Specialist, prepare as though you are a Specialist. You can always move from a specialized job or career into a more general field. The opposite move—from the general to specific—is far more difficult without additional education.

Personality Type

How comfortable you feel about direct contact with people determines your personality type. You are an *Extrovert* if you like frequent contact with many people; an *Introvert* if you are most comfortable in your own company and seek opportunities to be alone; an *Ambivert* (or "In-between-vert") if you prefer neither extreme, but enjoy a measure of both.

Extroverts are the socialites of the world. They need to have a lot of people around, and invariably boast an array of friends and acquaintances only slightly smaller than the local telephone book. Networking is natural for them, and they thrive on people contact. Extroverts even think out loud, often talking and acting before thoroughly thinking about what they're saying or doing. Full of energy, they are depressed when nothing is happening.

Extroverts run for student government, star in school plays, and become cheerleaders. They excel in careers that require them to be outgoing and action-oriented—jobs that call for an aggressive approach and involve extensive interaction with people. Extroverts, therefore, are "naturals" for most sales and promotion work.

Introverts are often perceived as quiet and reserved, even shy. At a party, an Introvert usually will converse with the one or two people they already know and feel comfortable with. On an airplane, two Introverts sitting in adjoining seats might not even exchange pleasantries.

Introverts are the class treasurers and secretaries, not the presidents. Studying provides a greater satisfaction than most social situations. Introverts enjoy jobs that allow them to work behind the scenes, away from the spotlight Extroverts crave. They like calm environments and time to think about things.

Extroverts and Introverts often fail to understand one another. Extroverts tend to view Introverts as bores with little zest for life, often misinterpreting their reserved natures as cold aloofness. Introverts, in turn, view Extroverts as shallow and impulsive, often dismissing them as impetuous and immature.

Ambiverts, as the name suggests, show less extreme preferences—most of them are not *extroverted* enough for sales, nor *introverted* enough for research and analysis positions. They are happy in jobs that give them a mix of people contact and solitary work.

One woman, who wrote and developed corporate training programs and then taught them to classes of 40 or 50 people, described her Ambivert quality as being 100 percent introverted while writing and 100 percent extroverted while teaching—neither of which would satisfy her 100 percent of the time.

Conceptualizing Aptitudes

The strength or weakness of your Conceptualizing Aptitudes determines how you produce ideas, organize them, and perceive relationships among them. They establish the way you evaluate problems and generate solutions to them. Imaginative or critical thinking indicate your strength in these aptitudes.

Pick An Idea, *Any* Idea

People who are naturally imaginative or creative possess **Strong Ideaphoria**. They excel at brainstorming; ideas—both good and bad—are readily available. Their rapid flow of thought makes them "lateral" rather than "linear" thinkers—straight line thinking is difficult; the scenic route is more to their liking.

People with strong Ideaphoria have a particularly low tolerance for routine, repetitious jobs that require a consistent way of doing things. Their short attention span demands a great deal of variety in their jobs, especially if there is little room for creativity. Injecting a new idea where one is not needed can lead to minor irritations and major financial problems. (One seasoned accountant remarked that there was a name for creative people in his profession—jailbirds.)

People with strong Ideaphoria often spend extensive time daydreaming. This trait is not exactly a plus in jobs that require a no-nonsense, cut-and-dried approach. In the right job or career, however, it *can* be—daydreams often produce fresh ideas with the imagery needed to attract attention.

Another characteristic of people with strong Ideaphoria is that they are very talkative—especially if they are very extroverted. Salespeople find this ability particularly useful—excelling at "small talk" is one key to establishing the friendly rapport necessary in most sales situations.

People with *Weak Ideaphoria* perform well in positions that require a consistent approach. Managers with weak Ideaphoria are less likely to change things or innovate. Their subordinates are often more productive because they are not constantly learning a new way to do things. Most people responsible for ongoing administrative functions benefit from weak Ideaphoria.

People with weak Ideaphoria *do* come up with good ideas. But instead of spontaneously generating ideas hither ,and yon, they tend to combine their experience and knowledge with existing ideas to make modest improvements, not wholesale changes. Their ideas tend to be rearrangements of old ones, not the unexpected concepts that spring full-blown from people with strong Ideaphoria.

The Man With The Plan

People with a *Strong Analytical* aptitude bring order to seemingly chaotic circumstances. They are skilled at making a schedule that can accomodate all the constraints imposed on it. Organizing, coordinating, and planning are relatively simple tasks for anyone with this aptitude.

Balancing complicated daily schedules demands strong Analytical aptitude. Many working mothers demonstrate such an ability. Scheduling car pools for the children, meetings with their teachers, lunches with important clients, time for household shopping, dates for professional meetings, and dinner parties for friends plus handling day-to-day responsbilities demands great organizational skill...or a full-time personal assistant!

If you have *Weak Analytical* aptitude, you must learn to compensate for it by becoming a more conscientious planner, allowing extra time to make out schedules, and putting extra effort into the planning phases of a project. Relying on others for solutions to complicated accounting or systems analysis problems may well be vital for survival. You may find it necessary to organize your physical surroundings so that losing things does not become a habit—a messy desk is a luxury *you* can't afford.

Elementary, My Dear Watson!

Diagnostic aptitude—the "detective aptitude"—characterizes individuals with the ability to draw conclusions from scattered bits and pieces of information. Strength in this aptitude enables you to handle people in a diplomatic way as you sense feelings intuited but not necessarily expressed. Negotiators and arbitrators find this skill essential to their careers. Generalists with a strong Diagnostic aptitude are particularly adept at surmising people's motives.

People with a *Strong Diagnostic* ability seem to automatically question situations and events. They are critical thinkers who readily see the downside in most situations. Often this knack for immediately seeing both pros and cons makes the person with strong Diagnostic aptitude indecisive.

People who must be patient and accepting with associates need a *Weak Diagnostic* aptitude. They are less critical in their dealings with people who struggle in their work—especially new hires just catching on. Managers with a weakness in this critical thinking aptitude are less likely to discourage their subordinates with caustic, negative remarks.

A person with strong Ideaphoria but very weak Analytical and Diagnostic aptitudes often struggles to organize his thinking. He seems a bit scatter-brained, even "flaky." Without average or strong talent in these organizational aptitudes, the person with abundant ideas will find it difficult to channel them in a productive way.

Performing Aptitudes

Do you find some tasks particularly easy? Others very difficult? Are you frustrated by the detail work necessary to turn an idea into reality? Or does such "dirty work" really satisfy you? Your answers to these questions reflect your *Performing Aptitudes.*

Any Decade Now

Foresight is the most general of the Performing Aptitudes. It determines how frequently you need feedback on your performance to avoid getting discouraged.

Individuals with **Weak Foresight** require constant feedback—they must *always* know how they are measuring up...today. They are likely to place greater value on *short-term* rewards and rapidly change direction if they encounter obstacles to their long-range goals.

Students with weak Foresight are likely to do poorly in courses that involve only midterm and final exams—they need weekly quizzes and some personal interaction with their teacher to stay motivated in a course. And they will change their majors or career plans when they confront a particularly difficult course or unusually irascible professor, spending more time making *new* plans than finding ways around the obstacles to their *old* ones.

An employee with weak Foresight needs more frequent performance reviews and will value several small raises a few months apart more than a large yearly raise. Salespeople with weak Foresight prefer a weekly draw or monthly commission to a yearly plan.

For the student with *Strong Foresight,* an unlikable teacher or hard course is not an insurmountable obstacle. This is one the reason that many such students earn graduate and professional degrees.

Salespeople with strong Foresight will look for long-term rewards—stock in the company, a good retirement plan, or profit sharing. A number of people with strong Foresight start their own companies, fully capable of surviving the present by focusing on future rewards.

Business owners or executives with strong Foresight make decisions based on their long-term implications, not just their immediate impact. Such willingness to embrace an idea's potential when the immediate rewards are minimal, even nonexistent, threatens executives with weak Foresight. If you are an executive with weak Foresight, you need strong support from strategic planners to help formulate long-term plans for the company.

Entrepreneurs need strong Foresight or powerful techniques to compensate for their lack of it, since most of them must work many years before their ideas turn a profit. Since few people just starting their ventures have the capital to afford strategic planners, they must be capable of formulating their own plans to achieve their long-term goals.

Weak Foresight does not indicate that long-term goals and strategic planning are impossible. It simply requires more conscious planning—putting long-range goals in writing and delineating the short-term steps necessary to achieve them.

Likewise, possessing strong Foresight doesn't mean you don't enjoy pats on the back and more tangible rewards as often as you can get them. We all like feedback. But it does mean that your job will be unfulfilling if it does not involve, to some extent, the pursuit of long-range goals.

What's Next, Teacher?

An individual with *Strong Perceptual Speed*—the "paperwork aptitude"—can fill out long forms and do calculations quickly, with a minimum of errors. Such students, for example, usually finish long multiple choice tests well ahead of the rest of the class.

Students with **Weak Perceptual Speed** often lose their places on computer-graded answer sheets and transpose numbers when making calculations. They do much better on untimed tests, where they can periodically go back to check their work for clerical errors.

Strong Perceptual Speed is an asset to accountants, secretaries, or any career that involves daily working with vast quantities of paperwork. The insurance and banking industries rely heavily on such people. People with weak Perceptual Speed will struggle with the entry-level office positions in these businesses, finding it stressful, even impossible, to be fast *and* accurate simultaneously.

People with weak Perceptual Speed should become used to inaccurate bank balances, unclaimed refunds, and tax penalties unless they learn to cope with their lack of this aptitude. These people function better by scheduling frequent, short periods of time to complete their paperwork or delegating as much of it as possible.

Your strength in Perceptual Speed will give you some idea of the amount of paperwork appropriate for your job. Average paperwork aptitude tells you that most jobs would not present a problem, but accounting, data processing, and similar jobs may be too much for you. If you are very weak in this aptitude and interview for a job that involves spending 80 percent of you time on paperwork, you would make a serious mistake if you accepted it.

Sometimes other strong aptitudes can "overpower" Perceptual Speed. A person with strong Ideaphoria, for example, cannot tolerate desk jobs that require routine work for long periods of time. Even *with* strong Perceptual Speed, this person will struggle to stay focused—his mind will wander and he will lose track of the details. An extremely extroverted person with strong Perceptual Speed will not be happy with most desk jobs either. With so many people around, she will be too distracted to function.

Because other aptitudes can so easily subjugate Perceptual Speed, you can, to some extent, decide how important a role you want this aptitude to play in any career decision.

You don't *have* to become an accountant just because you have strong Perceptual Speed. Most jobs require *some* sort of paperwork. If you have a lot of other aptitudes or special interests, you may wish to regard your paperwork aptitude as a secondary, or "helping," aptitude, not the primary one to use in your career.

Tell Me, Don't Show Me

Structural Visualization is an aptitude involving three dimensional sight—the ability to "see" buildings, machines, or other physical objects in your mind even though you cannot see them with your eyes.

This is not an aptitude that is readily usable in a lot of jobs or circumstances. In fact, unless you've taken college courses in such areas as architecture, mechanical engineering, or structural geology, you may have no idea about your talent—or lack of it—for such thinking. Students with *Strong Structural Visualization* who major in such areas as history, psychology, and finance might never realize their talent, as such disciplines never expose them to activities requiring this special ability.

Industries that employ people with strong Structural Visualization are construction, manufacturing, production, fabrication, medical, and agricultural People with positions in such areas as production management and materials handling are more likely to use strong Structural Visualization than those in the human resources management and public relations departments. The fact that more men than women are strong in this area is reflected in women's propensity to study law or business over medicine, engineering or science.

Salespeople can use this strong aptitude if they sell such products as biomedical equipment, industrial machinery, or scientific instruments. Products such as life insurance, financial services, and office supplies would not use it.

Interpreting a contour map or a blueprint takes more effort and time if you have *Weak Structural Visualization.* If you choose a business career that requires you to imagine things in three dimensions, be prepared to spend more time reading blueprints, investigating technical information, and checking specifications. As you move forward in your career, aim for a management track, not a technical one. Moving into the financial, personnel, or public relations department would also downplay your weakness.

Having strong Structural Visualization can present some problems, even if you are in an industry that is appropriate for your talent. As you move up the ladder, especially in a large company, you get further and further away from the tasks that enabled you to use this aptitude and more involved with budgets and personnel problems. If you move to the very top of the ladder, you become almost wholly concerned with financial information, economic trends, and corporate image.

If you find yourself unable to use one of the talents that propelled you to success in the beginning, you will need to find a way to channel this talent. Sometimes moving to a smaller company, where you will be in touch with the actual production, scientific, or technical work, can help. Hobbies that use strong Structural Visualization can also help—going on archaeological digs, designing and building furniture, etc.

If you have *Average Structural Visualization*, you may not have the talent to be an architect, but you are likely to enjoy work that involves a tangible product. If you wind up in sales, products that have a physical reality will attract you more than intangible products or services. You are likely to achieve more success if you sell airplanes or computers than financial services or radio/TV air time. If you are a loan officer at a bank, you will probably do better with clients in real estate and manufacturing businesses than with those in personnel placement and advertising.

Parlez Vous Francais?

Associative Memory is an aptitude for relating unfamiliar words to words you recognize in print. Students with strength in this aptitude find certain parts of foreign language study easy. They can quickly memorize foreign language vocabulary when they look at the words and see them paired with their English definitions. Memorizing scientific, medical, or legal terminology uses the same strong aptitude. Students with *Strong Associative Memory* are more successful than other students when they "cram" for a test.

Strong Associative Memory can be used in a variety of business pursuits—to pick up the jargon peculiar to different industries or acquire foreign language fluency for working overseas . It will also be helpful dealing with clients from other countries, in import/export businesses, or managing workers in this country who have not mastered English.

If you have *Weak Associative Memory* and need to learn a foreign language vocabulary, reinforce yourself by saying the words out loud, listening to tape recordings in the foreign language, and writing the words in your own handwriting. Remember that this aptitude pertains to looking at the words *in print* and remembering them; it has very little to do with *hearing* them or *speaking* the language.

I'm Going to Bloomies

Design Memory is another type of visual memory ability, used to remember the lines in a design. Biology students with *Strong Design Memory,* for example, find it easier to memorize what different types of cells look like. Those taking electronics or electrical engineering courses are good at remembering how circuits are designed. Those taking Art Appreciation can easily remember and identify individual works of art. Students with *Weak Design Memory* simply spend more time when they memorize different design features.

Businesses that produce or market design-oriented products—apparel, home furnishings, shoes, jewelry, art objects, antiques, real estate, etc.—offer opportunities to the person with an ability to remember design detail. Buyers who must recall differences in the design features of similar products can use this talent, as can systems analysts working with flow charts.

If you are weak in this aptitude, make notes or sketches for yourself when you must remember specific design features. If you are strong in it but have no outlets in your job, develop hobbies that use it— art appreciation courses, collecting art or antiques, learning to identify different types of plants, collecting coins or stamps, flower arranging, or designing and maintaining an aquarium.

Just Call Me AT&T

Number Memory is an aptitude for seeing and remembering numerical information, a helpful one to have in a society as numerically-oriented as ours: We have numbers for bank accounts, insurance policies, student identification, social security, credit cards, driver's license, warranties, etc.

Students with **Strong Number Memory** can easily recall a date for a history exam, numbers for a mathematical or chemistry formula, and all the digits for all their friends' telephone numbers. Shoppers who compare prices for the same item at different stores do not have to write down the information if they have strong Number Memory.

This is a helpful aptitude in jobs that require memorizing prices and quantities of things. Before most stockbrokers had ready access to computer terminals, they relied on strong Number Memory to keep tabs on financial information that changed every day. People working in purchasing, inventory control, and order processing benefit from a talent for remembering numbers. Work in accounting and finance offers some opportunities for using strong Number Memory.

If you have **Weak Number Memory** aptitude, don't be too concerned. Most businesses have computerized their quantitative data and make it readily available to most employees. Keeping your personal numbers organized at home on a computer or in an up-to-date file will save you time if it is hard for you to remember numbers. If you have a sensitive family, be sure to include birthdays and anniversaries in your personal file and look at it every couple of weeks to see what's coming up. When you reach executive level, perhaps your secretary will manage your number file for you.

Mr. Fixit To The Rescue

Finger Dexterity and **Instrument Dexterity** are aptitudes for manipulating small objects. Finger Dexterity involves working directly with the hands; Instrument

Dexterity involves using small tools. Some people have strong talent in both; some in one but not the other; still others in neither. If you work quickly and easily with your hands, stop to think about whether you perform best when you work with tiny instruments, such as tweezers, or when you use your fingers.

Children with good dexterities usually enjoy making models, cutting and pasting paper, building with blocks, and using play tools. Music students with good dexterities have an advantage with certain instruments, especially piano. The chemistry student with good dexterities drops fewer test tubes. People with good dexterities are more adept at connecting jewelry clasps and sewing on buttons and are attracted to crafts and other hobbies that use their hands. Some even fiddle with paper clips and pencils if their hands are not otherwise occupied.

On the other hand, if you always drop things in the kitchen, cut yourself shaving, hit the wrong keys on your calculator, and mess up small repair jobs, you probably have poor dexterities.

Don't worry. Weak Finger or Instrument Dexterity is a very minor problem in most business occupations. If you are working at a computer keyboard, word processor, or calculator all day, of course, it *will* have an effect on how fast you do your work. But the more you practice, the faster you'll perform. If you can delegate the data entry parts of your work as you move up, you can avoid any problems.

If you have strong dexterities and no work activity that uses them, there are hundreds of hobbies from which to choose. Gourmet cooking, carpentry, sewing, making jewelry, gardening, playing a musical instrument, repairing small motors, and knitting are a few examples.

Why Is The Dog Howling?

Pitch Discrimination is the most interesting of the music aptitudes because it has surprising applications *outside* the field of music.

Strong Pitch Discrimination is an obvious asset in singing and playing the guitar and any other situations that require the listener to hear very small differences in pitch. For some reason, this talent is also typical of people who can discriminate very small differences with their senses of sight and touch.Photographers who must judge lighting extremely well and focus their cameras quickly and precisely are one example. People who buy fine fabrics use this aptitude when judging minute differences in textures. Laboratory workers who weigh and measure materials with great precision use it, too.

So Pitch Discrimination can really be described as a *precision* aptitude. It could be used in certain types of quality control jobs that call for very close tolerances. People lacking Pitch Discrimination must depend on mechanical or electronic instruments rather than their own senses of sight, hearing, and touch for precise measurements.

Tonal Memory is an aptitude for remembering melodies and for playing by ear. People who have strength in this aptitude can hum a tune or pick it out on the piano after hearing it only once. Tonal Memory and Pitch Discrimination are the most important aptitudes for most muscial performing careers.

Time Discrimination and *Rhythm Memory* have applications in sports and dancing as well as in musical performance. Time Discrimination has to do with sensing tempo and repetitious patterns. Good skeet shooters and race car drivers have *Strong Time Discrimination.*

Rhythm Memory has to do with remembering more complicated patterns of sound. Good drummers are talented in both aptitudes.

People with these aptitudes are attracted to sports and cheerleading in school. They usually enjoy dancing, and they have more natural ability in sports than other people. People lacking a strong sense of rhythm and time spend more time practicing and find it difficult to change pace in the middle of a game or dance.

Timbre Discrimination is an aptitude for hearing "tone quality" or overtones. A person with *Strong Timbre Discrimination* is likely to override other voices when singing with a choral group; one with *Weak Timbre Discrimination* will blend in. Opera singers, public speakers, and radio and television announcers who can easily modulate their voices to be rich and pleasing to other people usually have strong Timbre Discrimination. Those with weak aptitude in this area must work harder at breathing properly and projecting their voices when they speak.

Loudness Discrimination involves hearing very small differences in the softness and loudness of tones. It is a more important aptitude for musicians performing classical music than for those performing rock and roll. It is also an important aptitude for audio engineers. The public relations person in charge of an important news conference might use this aptitude to make sure the electronic equipment is properly adjusted. The talent agent might use it to judge the ability of a singer or musician. You might use it to balance your stereo speakers.

Musical aptitudes can be used in businesses connected to music publishing, sound recording, broadcasting, concert production, musical instrument retailing, motion picture and video production, entertainment, and the areas of advertising that use the electronic media.

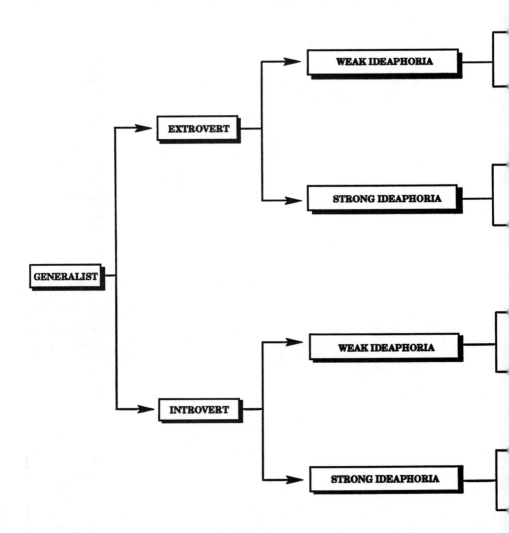

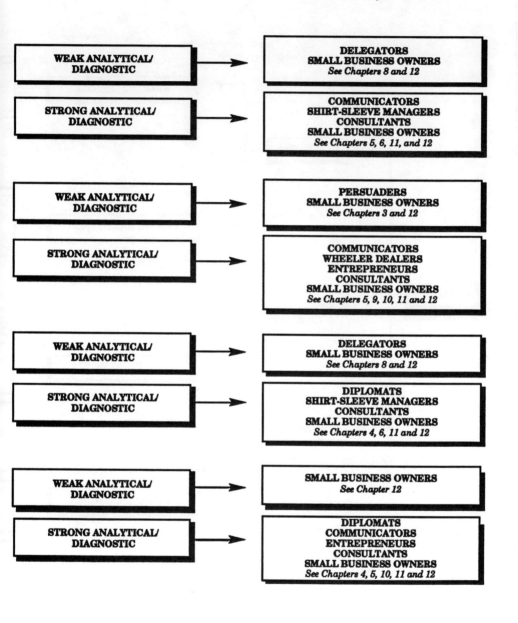

WEAK ANALYTICAL/
DIAGNOSTIC → **DELEGATORS**
SMALL BUSINESS OWNERS
See Chapters 8 and 12

STRONG ANALYTICAL/
DIAGNOSTIC → **COMMUNICATORS**
SHIRT-SLEEVE MANAGERS
CONSULTANTS
SMALL BUSINESS OWNERS
See Chapters 5, 6, 11, and 12

WEAK ANALYTICAL/
DIAGNOSTIC → **PERSUADERS**
SMALL BUSINESS OWNERS
See Chapters 3 and 12

STRONG ANALYTICAL/
DIAGNOSTIC → **COMMUNICATORS**
WHEELER DEALERS
ENTREPRENEURS
CONSULTANTS
SMALL BUSINESS OWNERS
See Chapters 5, 9, 10, 11 and 12

WEAK ANALYTICAL/
DIAGNOSTIC → **DELEGATORS**
SMALL BUSINESS OWNERS
See Chapters 8 and 12

STRONG ANALYTICAL/
DIAGNOSTIC → **DIPLOMATS**
SHIRT-SLEEVE MANAGERS
CONSULTANTS
SMALL BUSINESS OWNERS
See Chapters 4, 6, 11 and 12

WEAK ANALYTICAL/
DIAGNOSTIC → **SMALL BUSINESS OWNERS**
See Chapter 12

STRONG ANALYTICAL/
DIAGNOSTIC → **DIPLOMATS**
COMMUNICATORS
ENTREPRENEURS
CONSULTANTS
SMALL BUSINESS OWNERS
See Chapters 4, 5, 10, 11 and 12

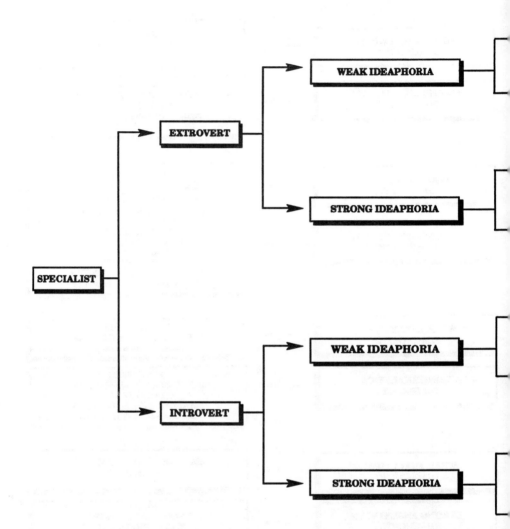

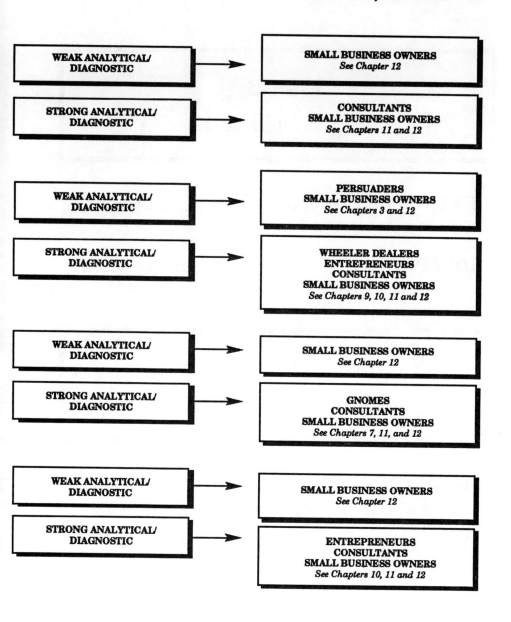

EXTROVERT *An outgoing, sociable, somewhat impulsive personality*

IDEAPHORIA *An imaginative or creative ability useful in generating a rapid flow of ideas and brain-storming*

ANALYTICAL *A methodical type of problem-solving ability useful in organizing, coordinating, and planning*

DIAGNOSTIC *An intuitive type of problem-solving ability helpful in investigation and research*

PERCEPTUAL SPEED *The ability to perform computational and clerical work quickly and accurately*

Three

The Persuaders

"Personality plus," words that epitomize Persuaders.

Suzy has an enviable sales reputation—she can, legend has it, sell snowsuits to Tahitians and bikini underwear to 300-pound men. Suzy is what most sales managers call a "natural"...as they start drooling over the thought of hiring her away.

Suzy can't help it. By sheer force of personality, she presents ideas in an exciting and memorable way. Her friends describe her as a "fun" person, "because she never meets a stranger." Suzy, and Persuaders like her, *always* makes an impression.

A drama major, Suzy had set her sights on a career as an actress or television personality. For many, such dreams tend to crumble right after graduation, when the reality of the competition, heartbreak and failure rate in the entertainment industry sets in. Suzy wound up selling advertising space in the *Yellow Pages*, a "get-by," short-term job, she was sure.

It turned out to be the steppingstone to her successful sales career. Trying to sell an ad to the director of marketing for the city's cultural arts council, she was hired instead.

Recognizing Suzy's selling abilities, the marketing director offered her a position with the city's performing arts groups. The idea of being involved with the orchestra and playhouse thrilled her, and she immediately accepted.

Today Suzy solicits grants, donations, volunteers, and free goods and services from a wide variety of companies and individuals. She is most effective when she has an opportunity to socially interact with potential donors, establishing the kind of rapport that ultimately opens their wallets.

The arts take on a new flair because of Suzy's sales presentations, and Suzy has thrived in a job and atmosphere that lets her use all her creative energies and talents. Combined with her sincere personality, they enable her to disarm even the wariest potential donors—Suzy always has reasonable answers to their objections.

Suzy is a typical Persuader, an individual whose natural aptitudes easily influence and motivate people. These abilities often make Persuaders like Suzy naturals at sales, where their strong Extrovert and Ideaphoria aptitudes only contribute to their performance and success. The typical Persuader's weak Analytical and Diagnostic abilities—which make her positive, enthusiastic and uncritical—actually work to her advantage in a sales position.

People such as Suzy are usually top producers who are highly recruited by marketing directors, sales managers, and business owners. These wallet-waving employers literally drool over the possibility of hiring such "naturals" who require little or no training in interpersonal skills. Extrovert Persuaders often need only to familiarize themselves with the product they're supposed to sell before hitting the road...and outselling the veterans.

Extroverts don't just *enjoy* frequent contact with people, they find such interaction positively stimulating and almost *essential* to their natures. The numerous in-person calls any successful salesperson must make daily, weekly and monthly don't intimidate the Extrovert, as they might an Introvert or Ambivert. On the contrary, many Extroverts thrive in situations that *require* several contacts daily.

Can Shy People Sell?

The "natural" salesperson may be an Extrovert, but that doesn't mean Introverts needn't apply, just that they need to carefully seek sales jobs in which the high-octane personality they lack is *not* a major requirement. Retail (inside) sales is such an opportunity, in which the steady flow of customers requires attention and service, not high pressure selling. If a popular product is in short supply, even an *outside* salesperson has to do little but make sure his accounts know how to contact him. Wherever heavy demand and limited supply is the norm, Introverts can excel.

Introverts can also excel in the world of "old money"— that rarified stratum of families that have been wealthy for generations. Such individuals often feel uncomfortable with talkative, action-oriented Extroverts, even refusing to buy if they think they are being pushed. But they are right at home with an Introvert.

Look For The Soft Sell

Ambiverts in sales and promotion are most productive when *servicing* established accounts is as important as *creating* new ones and a "soft" sell is better than a "hard" one.

April explains how her Ambivert personality turned out to be her biggest asset when she took a job selling wholesale food products:

> A "hard" sell in this business—and a hard-charging salesperson—is really out of place. The restaurants, cafeterias, schools, and hospitals I service *have* to buy food from *some*one. I don't have to identify or establish the need for my product, usually the first step in any selling situation. It's already obvious.

What *is* important is making sure that the orders are accurately communicated to headquarters and delivered on time. The quality of the food, the dependability of delivery, and competitive pricing keep established accounts for the company.

The fact that the food company did not have very many competitors in her region didn't hurt—and made the job even more suitable for a service-oriented Ambivert like April.

Generalists Vs. Specialists

Persuaders with a Generalist frame of reference tend to be better suited to sales and promotion positions than Specialists. They should seek to represent a wide array of products and call on many different types of clients.

An insurance agent, who must guide companies and individuals through an increasingly complex maze of insurance choices for both individuals and companies, is a good example of the right job for a Generalist Persuader. Being on the same "wave length" as most other people enables the agent to communicate with a wide *variety* of clients while addressing each of their *specific* needs. And the broad range of available insurance products is compatible with the Generalist's tendency to excel in areas that require a little knowledge about a lot of things.

Specialist Persuaders

Because of their unique outlooks, Specialist Persuaders encounter obstacles that Generalists would walk over without even noticing. Since they do not see things the way most people do, Specialists trying to sell a wide array of products to many different kinds of people are in for a struggle. In fact, extroverted Specialists often project a prima donna image that further undermines their ability to relate to many of their clients.

Specialist Persuaders succeed in sales situations in which a narrowly-defined market or a highly-specialized product allow them to become experts. Rather than working with discounted items that require high-volume selling, the Specialist should seek a position selling high-ticket items, in which expertise is more important than personality.

A second factor important to Specialists is the flexibility of the organization. Specialists in sales are frequently trapped by organizational friction. If the corporate culture militates against a rather independent approach to sales, the Specialist will feel that his productivity is being thwarted by the company.

The company's bureaucracy may be intolerant of their free-spirited approach, interpreting it as contempt for rules and policy. When selecting a company, the Specialist needs to choose one that encourages him to function independently.

Sam, a Specialist, did everything right. After getting his degree in finance, he chose a young commercial real estate firm that was interested in results and evolved a sales technique that matched his brusque "let's get down to business" attitude. Sam rapidly developed a narrow expertise— selling and leasing warehouses—such that other brokers just as quickly came to regard him as the "warehouse man." They knew he could find exactly what their clients needed, even when those needs were peculiar. Having earned a reputation and built his niche, Sam got rich on the commissions.

Complementary Weak Aptitudes

Ironically, a typical Persuader's weak aptitudes significantly contribute to his sales ability—sometimes as much or more than his strong aptitudes.

The Persuader with weak Perceptual Speed—the "paperwork aptitude"—avoids desk duty with characteristic zeal. Given a choice between paperwork and sales calls, a typical Persuader will readily dive into the latter.

Too much involvement with paperwork dampens the salesperson's need for activity. A common observation among salespeople, sales managers, and business owners is that the best salespeople are sloppy, inaccurate, and tardy with their reports and allergic to their desks.

Smart bosses find it more profitable to engineer a system that requires minimal paperwork from their salespeople. They would much prefer to hire additional clerical support for their high-flying Persuaders than to force them to write extensive reports or replace them with salespeople who like clerical tasks...and sell less.

A manager of an office equipment company recounts her experience with a sales representative who had extremely *strong* Perceptual Speed:

> I'll never forget Mike. He made a fantastic first impression when he interviewed for the job, and I thought he'd be great at getting us some new business. I just knew he had it in him. I could picture him strolling into offices, laying on that charm, and getting those sales contracts signed.
>
> Mike was an utter disappointment. He'd make one or two calls a day, then come back to the office to shoot the bull with whoever happened to be here. He used that sparkling personality of his, all right, but not on customers!
>
> The straw that broke the camel's back was when I found out he was doing the paperwork for the other sales reps. Most of them slave over the forms for twenty or thirty minutes, but it only took Mike ten minutes to turn one out. Then he could tell jokes and generally have a good time. He didn't make enough sales calls, and he kept the others from theirs. He distracted my office help as well.
>
> I sat down with Mike and explained that we did not pay salary plus commission and give him a car with a phone so he could spend half his day at the office. I told him the only time he needed to do paperwork was when he wrote up a sales contract on a piece of equipment he himself sold.
>
> He shaped up for a while after that, but I had to let him go the day he took it upon himself to assist the inventory people sent in from headquarters to do an item count. They were mostly young women, and Mike managed to turn their job into a form of recreation by helping them locate, count, and tabulate things in between his stand-up comic routine. This type of work makes no difference at all when I report my group's total sales at the end of the month.
>
> Mike might be a wonderful guy to everybody else, but he máde me look bad every time I sent in the sales reports. So it was "so long, Mike."

Mike's strong Perceptual Speed diminished his drive to be away from the office. As long as he could create situations to satisfy his need for interaction with people at the office, he felt no compelling urge to contact prospective clients.

If Mike eventually realizes the casualties of the tug of war between his Perceptual Speed and his selling talent, he could change his behavior and become a topflight sales representative.

Critical Minds Don't Sell

Weak Analytical and Diagnostic aptitudes also benefit the Persuader, since these are "thinking" rather than "doing" aptitudes. The highly analytical salesperson, like the paperwork-oriented one, has a propensity to spend too much time preparing reports and making plans. Customers are not contacted. Sales not made.

The person with weak Diagnostic aptitude is slow to spot pitfalls and see disadvantages. Strength in this ability becomes a problem when the salesperson perceives why the customer should *not* buy and even starts explaining his product's defects to prospective buyers. Some salespeople with strong Diagnostic aptitude talk themselves out of their sales before they even see the customers, anticipating customers' objections...and *agreeing* with them!

The critical thinker typically lacks the patience with people and hand-holding essential to success in consumer-oriented sales. Those of you who aspire to sales careers but are cursed with strong Diagnostic or Analytical aptitude should seek positions that require rather technical or sophisticated knowledge and allow you to act as consultants working to solve your clients' needs.

Jessica's story illustrates why many critical thinkers fail in sales careers. She gained notoriety by telling customers all the drawbacks of the cars she showed them. After highlighting the features of a particular model, Jessica brought up the possible problems each buyer might encounter.

A young couple interested in a sports car got a lecture about its impracticality for anyone who planned to have children in the near future. The same couple heard about the low gas mileage for station wagons and the discomfort of subcompacts on road trips.

Frequently salespeople at neighboring dealerships found these educated consumers willing buyers—especially if they had seen Jessica the same day. The customers wanted to feel good about their decisions. Jessica made them think they were making bad decisions. Her competitors said nothing to undermine the customers' willingness to buy.

When her sales manager confronted her, Jessica merely told him that she had no respect for people who were not willing to look at the good points and bad points and make up their own minds.

"I'm not going to stand there and tell them they're doing the right thing and coax them into a car they think is perfect," she informed him. "*No* car is perfect. They might like to *think* it is, and they might resent me when I tell them the trouble spots. But that's *their* problem. If they can't make a decision to buy, I'm not going to make it for them."

Needless to say, Jessica now has an opportunity to find a new job, hopefully a sales position that will put a premium on her educating a client and not persuading them to buy.

If you are a Persuader with strong Analytical or Diagnostic aptitudes, the Communicator jobs described in Chapter 5 might be more appropriate career choices (though you should look for the more aggressive positions that will suit your extroverted personality).

When Persuaders Fail

Sam in real estate and Suzy in the arts are typical Persuaders successful in sales and promotion positions, but failures like Jessica *do* exist. Why do some Persuaders fail at jobs that would seem custom-tailored to their personalities?

Starting a career in a sedentary job that requires the Persuader to suppress his natural tendency for talking, socializing, and moving about causes failure for some. Secretarial and administrative support positions are poison to such active people. One Houston woman recounted her experience with a firm that sold advertising specialty items:

> They told me I could have a crack at sales if I'd agree to an administrative support position first. This was supposed to acquaint me with the products and give me time to learn from the salespeople by assisting them with their paperwork. Well, I made so many mistakes that they fired me after only two months. I *know* I could have sold more than any of their other sales reps, but I'd lost my credibility by failing at paper pushing. So I never got the chance to *sell.*

A second pitfall for the Persuader is academia. Most sales positions have few specific educational or college major requirements. It is relatively easy and often advisable for Persuaders to forgo extended years of education. That's because the Persuader is already so well suited for sales that college will teach him little more.

Some Persuaders know themselves well enough to choose the active life of a salesperson, then fail because they do not acquire enough knowledge about their products or services. Emphasizing activity and personality over competency propels many Persuaders to ruin.

It's relatively easy for a Persuader to use people skills and tap dance right out of a scene that may expose his lack of knowledge. However, even the *best* "con men" eventually get caught.

A Final Warning—Beware Promotions

The other reason Persuaders fail is a strange one— success in business usually leads to promotion. And promotion may be death to the active Persuader—the ranks of management seldom mesh with his aptitude profile. Persuaders find it difficult to be in the office and, not surprisingly, bosses, subordinates, and peers tend to get upset when the manager is never available.

Subordinates have a hard time regarding this talkative, friendly, and well-liked person as one who has the authority to reprimand and fire. And our Persuader manager procrastinates when the time comes to complete employee performance reviews. Then the boss and the subordinates are distraught at the same time.

If the Persuader manager doesn't resign, he usually gets fired. The business world is rife with stories of the company's best salesperson becoming its worst sales manager.

If you are a Persuader, beware of a management or administrative position. Think about your aptitudes and your need to be active. That management position might look like a promotion to your spouse, your colleagues, and your company. Make sure it doesn't look like a prison to *you*.

Elements Of Success

There are some other characteristics of successful salespeople that have nothing to do with the Persuader's aptitudes. One is that they believe in their products or services. Few successful salespeople sell things they hold in low regard. If you are seriously considering a sales career, choose a product that genuinely interests you.

Another characteristic of successful salespeople unrelated to aptitudes is that they sell to people who are very much like themselves. They and their clients have similar socio-economic backgrounds, and it is easy for them to understand each other. The comfort level in dealing with people who share your values and cultural characteristics is higher. As a result, it is easier to respond to their needs and desires.

Finally, most successful salespeople have strong ego drives. They are competitive. Making a sale means *winning*, and not making a sale means *losing*. When they lose, they have a burning desire to overcome defeat by making a sale the next time. They derive not only income but also ego satisfaction from selling.

Persuader Checkpoints

If you have strong Analytical and Diagnostic aptitudes and do *not* want them to impede your career in sales and promotion:

- Select a rather sophisticated product or service
- Educate and consult with your client
- Emphasize commercial accounts instead of direct sales to consumers
- Select a product or service for which a need already exists in the minds of your clients

If You Are A Generalist

- Sell or promote a wide variety of products or services
- Develop a diverse clientele
- Choose a company that emphasizes teamwork and daily interaction with other departments in the organization
- Emphasize your company's reputation

If You Are A Specialist

- Choose a specialized product or service with a high dollar value
- Concentrate on a specific type of client
- Find a company that encourages its salespeople to take an independent approach.
- Emphasize your strong personal reputation

If You Are An Extrovert

Look for sales and promotion positions that allow you to:
- Sell outside the office or store
- Make a large number of sales calls
- Create a large number of new accounts
- Close sales quickly
- Delegate paperwork to someone else

If You Are An Introvert

Look for sales and promotion positions that allow you to:
- Sell inside the office or store
- Avoid "cold calls"
- Serve existing accounts instead of creating new ones
- Meet a heavy demand for a scarce product or service
- Deal with "old money" clientele

If You Are An Ambivert

Look for sales and promotion positions that allow you to:
- Spend equal amounts of time on outside sales calls and office work
- Serve established accounts as well as create new ones
- Use a "soft" rather than a "hard" selling technique
- Emphasize continuing relationships with clients instead of quick closes

Persuaders Fail When They:

- Take entry-level desk jobs that emphasize paperwork ability instead of sales ability
- Do not acquire adequate knowledge of their products or services
- Accept promotion into the ranks of management

Persuaders Succeed When They:

- Believe in their products or services
- Sell to people very much like themselves
- Have strong ego drives

Persuader Business Careers

Account executive 164.167-010

Advertising account executive

Advertising sales representative 254.357-014

Aircraft sales representative 273.253-010

Apparel trimmings sales representative (wholesale trade) 261.357-010

Automotive leasing sales representative 273.357-014

Barber and beauty equipment and supplies sales representative (wholesale trade) 275.357-010

Business services sales representative 251.357-010

Canvas products sales representative (wholesale trade) 261.357-014

Church furniture and religious supplies sales representative (wholesale trade) 275.357-014

Commercial equipment and supplies sales representative (wholesale trade) 275.357-018

Communication equipment sales representative (wholesale trade) 271.257-010

Containers sales representative (wholesale trade) 274.357-026

Demonstrator 297.354-010

Education courses sales representative 259.257-010

Electronic parts sales representative (wholesale trade) 271.357-010

Exhibit-display representative 297.367-010

Field representative (wholesale trade) 163.267-010

Financial report service sales agent 251.357-014

Financial services sales representative 251.257-010

Floor coverings salesperson (wholesale trade) 270.357-026

Florist supplies sales representative (wholesale trade) 275.357-054

Food products sales representative (wholesale trade) 260.357-014

Footwear sales representative (wholesale trade) 261.357-018

Franchise sales representative 251.357-022

Fund raiser 293.157-010

General merchandise sales representative (wholesale trade) 279.357-014

Goodwill ambassador 293.357-018

Group insurance special agent 169.167-050

Group sales representative (amusement and recreation) 259.357-010

Hobbies and crafts sales representative (wholesale trade) 277.357-010

Home furnishings sales representative (wholesale trade) 270.357-010

Horticultural and nursery products salesperson (wholesale trade) 272.357-022

Hotel and restaurant equipment and supplies sales representative (wholesale trade) 275.357-026

Household appliances sales representative (wholesale trade) 270.357-014

Insurance sales agent 250.257-010

Insurance special agent 166.167-046

Jewelry sales representative (wholesale trade) 279.357-018

Leasing agent (real estate) 250.357-014

Leather goods sales representative (wholesale trade) 279.357-022

Livestock sales representative 260.257-010

Lobbyist 165.017-010

Manufacturers' representative
(nontechnical) 279.157-010

Membership solicitor 293.357-022

Men's and boy's apparel sales
representative (wholesale trade)
261.357-022

Motor vehicle and supplies sales
representative (wholesale trade)
273.357-022

Musical instruments and accessories sales
representative (wholesale trade)
277.357-014

Novelties sales representative (wholesale
trade) 277.357-018

Office machines sales representative
(wholesale trade)) 275.357-034

Outside sales representative

Paper and paper products sales
representative (wholesale trade)
279.357-026

Personnel recruiter 166.267-010

Plastic products sales representative
(wholesale trade) 279.357-030

Printing supplies sales representative
(wholesale trade) 274.357-062

Product representative 096.121-014

Promoter

Publications sales representative (wholesale
trade) 277.357-022

Publicity agent

Real estate guide 297.667-010

Real estate sales agent 250.357-018

Recreation and sporting goods sales
representative (wholesale trade)
277.357-026

Sales promotion representative (wholesale
trade) 269.357-018

Sales-service promoter 165.167-010

School equipment and supplies sales
representative (wholesale trade)
275.357-042

Song plugger (radio and television
broadcasting) 165.157-010

Textiles sales representative (wholesale
trade) 261.357-030

Trade show representative 297.367-010

Training representative 166.227-010

Vending and coin machines sales
representative (wholesale trade)
275.357-050

Veterinarian supplies sales representative
(wholesale trade) 276.357-018

Women's and girl's apparel sales
representative (wholesale trade)
261.357-038

Professional and Trade Groups

American Advertising Federation

American Association of Advertising
Agencies

American Marketing Association

Association of National Advertisers

The Bureau of Salesmen's National
Associations

Business/Professional Advertising
Association

Direct Selling Association

Independent Insurance Agents of America

Insurance Information Institute

Manufacturers' Agents National Association

Manufacturers' Representatives of America

National Association for Professional Saleswomen

National Association of Corporate and Professional Recruiters

National Association of Realtors

National Society of Sales Training Executives

Professional Salespersons of America

Sales and Marketing Executives International

Women in Advertising and Marketing

Women in Sales

Professional Reading

Ad Forum

Advertisers & Their Agencies

Advertising Age

Adweek

Agency Sales Magazine

The American Salesman

Direct Marketing

Food & Beverage Marketing

Geyer's Office Dealer

Incentive

Office Products Dealer

Opportunity

Personal Selling Power

Real Estate Today

Rough Notes

Sports Marketing News

GENERALIST *A frame of reference common to most people that facilitates coordination and compromise with others and emphasizes interpersonal skills*

ANALYTICAL *A methodical type of problem-solving ability useful in organizing, coordinating, and planning*

DIAGNOSTIC *An intuitive type of problem-solving ability helpful in investigation and research*

EXTROVERT *An outgoing, sociable, somewhat impulsive personality*

STRUCTURAL VISUALIZATION *The ability to visualize structures in three dimensions*

Four

The Diplomats

Frank, a typical Diplomat, performs magic...or at least seems to. It usually happens at company meetings when hotheads clash before, during and after dinner, or during union negotiations, or in public relations crises.

What's Frank's magic act? He has the uncanny ability to see all sides of a question and understand the personal motivations of each answer's champions.

And he listens a lot.

Almost without being aware of it, his mind pieces together all the divergent and seemingly-unrelated bits of information about people and events that it's stored away. Then, at the critical moment, he draws on this storehouse, adds a large dose of intuition, and offers a unique and creative solution to a seemingly intractable problem.

It was just this sort of incident that launched his quick climb up the corporate ladder.

Frank's company, an avionics concern heavily dependent on government contracts, employs union labor for assembly operations. It rotates its management trainees from department to department to give them knowledge of the whole company.

During Frank's management stint with the human resources department, he began attending contract negotiations between managers and union leaders. His boss, Sterling, was one of management's representatives at these meetings and thought it would be good training for Frank. As it turned out, Frank did more than his boss or anyone else to foster an agreement.

Here's how it happened: Larry was a company employee who had been instrumental in unionizing its production workers 20 years earlier. The local workers demanded his presence at the meeting because they knew he wouldn't "sell out." Lacking a formal education and strong communication skills, Larry felt intimidated in the presence of these well-educated managers. This insecurity and the pressure from his co-workers resulted in his stubborn, almost childish, refusal to modify the union's initial demand for a 20-percent pay raise.

Frank sympathized with the workers need to feel that they were getting ahead. Company profits had climbed steadily, and more orders were coming in from private airplane manufacturers. He agreed with union representatives that the production workers had contributed to the company's increased profits and deserved some of the rewards.

However, he also realized that a strike or an unmotivated work force would undermine the company's growth—not to mention that a 20-percent pay hike would wipe out a huge chunk of the profits. Ignoring stockholder interests and failing to retain enough capital to remain competitive certainly would hurt the company's long-term prospects.

This was information available to everyone. But Frank added his own understanding of the personal motives of Larry and Sterling.

Sterling, the son of one of the company's founders, had been shuffled off into the human resources department when it was still called "Personnel" and considered the stepchild among the company's departments.

He had made no outstanding contributions during his 15-year tenure there, and Frank had heard offhand remarks from some of the other managers about Sterling's lack of achievement. As one of them put it, "He's like a piece of antique furniture. They don't really want to get rid of him, but they certainly don't want to put him where they'll trip over him."

Should Sterling leave the meetings looking ineffectual, without making a distinctive contribution, any remaining credibility and stature would be lost. This was *his* "secret" agenda.

Larry had his own secret agenda—his strongest personal desire was to give his children the education he'd never had. During a brief encounter at the company picnic, Frank recalled Larry saying, "You know, that's why I keep at it, going to the plant every day. I'm going to see that my kids get an education. That's one thing nobody can ever take away from them."

From this seemingly off-hand remark, Frank understood that Larry was not the "unmovable" rock his negotiating tactics would lead one to believe—he and his fellow workers simply held higher hopes for their children than they held for themselves. This, it seemed to him, was the *real* motive behind the workers' seemingly-intractable desire for a 20% wage increase.

During one of the recesses, Frank suggested to Sterling a company-sponsored scholarship and a low-interest educational loan program for employees' children in lieu of part of the pay raise. This approach would not require immediate funding, and it would give Larry and other union members some of the security they sought. With Sterling's approval, Frank researched other companies' programs. A few days later, Sterling proposed the college scholarship and financial aid package—along with summer internships for college students who were the children of union members.

Sterling also presented another of Frank's suggestions—an in-house training program in electronics technology for the workers themselves. An arrangement with the local community college would give college credit for these courses. Larry found these proposals—along with an *eight*-percent pay increase—acceptable.

It Just Looks Like ESP

Frank's role in the union negotiations is representative of the way a typical Diplomat functions in many business situations. Diplomats like Frank work behind the scenes. The Diplomat's combination of strong reasoning skills (strong Analytical and Diagnostic aptitudes) and Generalist outlook result in a powerful ability to understand the motivations of other people and use that insight to solve "people problems."

Another factor in Frank's success—directly a result of his Diagnostic aptitude—was his recognition that Sterling was completely out of touch with Larry's concerns. Sterling felt Larry had achieved a great triumph because of the local union members' insistence on his presence at the contract negotiations. In Sterling's eyes, Larry was a true leader, one who held the esteem of his co-workers—the very things that Sterling desperately wished for himself.

Sterling's envy made him adamant in his positions as he sought to protect his fragile reputation, expecting that management would see any "softness" on his part as abject failure. But Sterling's efforts to save face came off as snobbery to Larry. In Larry's eyes, Sterling had everything—position, security, and education—all the things *he'd* never have, but perhaps could provide for his children. A 20-percent pay raise would go a long way toward securing his dreams.

Circumstances and personalities such as this often demand a mediator. Here is where the Diplomat has his greatest impact, operating as a conciliator bringing two factions together. Where clashing personalities and motives thwart compromise, Diplomats like Frank play the integral role in any settlement—bringing very divergent points of view to a common meeting ground acceptable to all.

The Games People Play

A final aspect of the Diplomat profile is its uncanny ability to navigate the political currents within the corporate structure. Most Diplomats play the corporate political game skillfully. It's easy for them to see what is important to others and where their interests fit into the overall scheme.

Frank—aware of Sterling's sensitivities and his position in a company that put a premium on nepotism—made a conscious decision to let Sterling have all the glory for the union settlement. As a result, when Frank asked Sterling to use his influence to get him transferred to the corporate communications department, Sterling readily paid his political debt. In doing so, he removed the one person in his department who represented a threat to his new and improved image. Sterling was appeased, and Frank's lateral move was the springboard for his own rapid rise in the company.

Diplomats play the corporate political game well, but they are not political in a glad-handing, smile-flashing way. If they run for political office in the public arena, for example, they have a difficult time making the required "larger-than-life" impressions on large crowds and television cameras.

The political abilities of Diplomats stem from their adept handling of people on a *one-to-one* basis, their ability to forge compromises, and their ability to fit each personal transaction into the "bigger picture." They usually maneuver out of harm's way in the midst of organizational struggles.

A Progress Report

Frank has climbed into a rather visible position, working closely with the top executives in marketing, finance, and production. His department prepares news releases, annual reports, and employee newsletters, the materials used in the company's in-house training programs, as well as the audio-visuals and printed matter used in proposals to clients.

Frank second-guesses the effects of information transmitted by the company and recommends how certain documents should be worded, when and how certain communications released.

Beyond these departmental responsibilities, the oligarchy running the company calls on Frank to observe whenever they anticipate a meeting with a preponderance of conflicts and communications problems. They now recognize that Frank's diplomacy in tense situations is one of his greatest assets for the company, making him an invaluable member of their team.

Obviously Frank's aptitudes have aided his career. As a Generalist, Frank is on the same "wave length" as most other people. His frame of reference facilitates his effective interaction with people of various backgrounds both in and out of the company.

Frank's strong Diagnostic aptitude helps him "read between the lines" when he observes people. It's second nature for him to correctly "guess" the motives of others. His strong Analytical aptitude helps him see how the pieces fit together, how one person's concerns can combine effectively with someone else's, and how this connection can be used to accomplish a task or to reach an agreement. Finally, his slightly introverted personality makes him a very capable listener, able to objectively weigh all sides of a controversy.

Frank thinks through problems thoroughly and does not present a solution until he has analyzed and criticized it in his own mind. He *always* thinks before he speaks. When he *does* talk, Frank presents his ideas in a straightforward, unadorned fashion.

The result is that people listen closely. He has an air of authority about him. When subordinates describe him, they do not use the word "friendly." "Respected" and "honorable" and "trustworthy" are more frequent descriptions.

Frank is weak in the Ideaphoria aptitude, but this is actually an asset in his work. A strong Ideaphoria aptitude denotes a rapid flow of sometimes unrelated ideas. Frank's job is to dissect and synthesize the ideas of others, *not* simply contribute even more ideas to the already-overflowing melting pot.

His weak Ideaphoria also helps him tolerate the ongoing administrative parts of his work. He does not create a new way to do things every day, and his subordinates are not bombarded with new projects before they finish the old ones.

Undiplomatic Careers

Frank used his political skills to get a position that fully utilized his Diplomatic aptitudes. Other Diplomats are not so lucky and drift into the wrong occupations. Lured by big money or by the fact that it's easy to get hired, they ignore their true talents.

The Call Of The Wild Buck

As a general rule Diplomats should not go into direct sales, as it is all too easy for them to become painfully aware of their products' drawbacks. When they have no compromises or modifications to offer the client, they find it a struggle to even call on him, much less persuade him to buy.

This critical thinking aptitude makes them critical of their products, critical of their customers, and critical of themselves—a deadly trinity in any sales career! The positive attitude that epitomizes great salespeople is simply not within the typical Diplomat.

Fay chose a sales career because her three closest college friends began making a lot of money quickly. All had gone into sales—one in real estate; another, securities; the third, insurance. Fay regarded them as real friends, but, deep down, she knew they were a bit flaky. She reasoned that if *they* could sell, *she* certainly could! How could they be making so much money while she was still looking for the right job?

So Fay took a job selling linen supply services to hospitals, hotels, and motels. Her company offered her a "ground floor opportunity" because it was a new enterprise. Fay was positive that she had the ability to make the most of that opportunity.

She could not have been more wrong!

Because Fay was an Introvert and weak in Ideaphoria, she lacked the personality and spontaneity necessary for direct sales. Cold calls were traumatic nightmares, not the opportunities they were to Persuaders. Small talk seemed silly to her. She suffered through the time spent with prospective clients—both she and her hapless prospects felt uncomfortable during her visits.

Not an auspicious start, but what sealed her failure were her strong Diagnostic and Analytical aptitudes. When a customer raised an objection, Fay often agreed with them!

When Fay got a noncommittal response to her first call on a prospect, she did not make a second call. She simply didn't have the patience for it. She knew it was time to quit the day she turned the car around and went home before she even got to a prospect's office, having already convinced herself that he wouldn't buy!

After this shining failure, Fay invested some time in introspection, thoroughly evaluating herself, her strengths, and her weaknesses. This eventually led her to a very successful career as a consumer affairs reporter, one that makes the most of her Diagnostic and Analytical aptitudes.

Some people who have failed as nobly as Fay in their first or second jobs neglect to look at themselves objectively and *learn* from their failures. Others can realistically analyze their abilities, but then rule out alternatives because they think they could not qualify for the right sort of job.

It might surprise you to know that most people with college diplomas do *not* end up working in fields directly related to their college majors. The circuitous nature of Fay's route to a successful business career typifies that of many liberal arts and social science majors.

When Sales *Isn't* Wrong

While it is common for Diplomats like Fay to make false starts in sales, other Diplomats find sales positions entirely appropriate for their talents. *These* sales jobs emphasize repeated contact with established customers and conscientious follow-up. Success does not depend on the creation of numerous new accounts.

In such a job, the product or service may be quite complicated, requiring the sales representative to spend a good deal of time teaching the customer. The ability to service an account has priority because of the complexity of the product or service or because of the importance of repeat sales. Most of the time, these sales positions involve selling to other businesses (business-to-business sales), *not* to individuals for personal consumption (direct sales).

Fred is a perfect example of a Diplomat who found a successful niche in sales. He represents several manufacturers of specialized metal clips and fasteners and calls on the manufacturing and fabrication companies that make products requiring these fasteners.

He doesn't ever have to sell hard. Sometimes he simply takes an order from a purchasing agent and makes sure that delivery is on time. With other customers, he listens to the reasons that a particular clip or fastener won't work on a new product. Then he makes an investigation of others that might work and presents the alternatives to the customer.

Fred does not have to create a need for his product in the minds of his customers. That need existed before Fred ever arrived on the scene. Fred's success depends on his follow through. His customers are aware of his efforts in their behalf because he meets their needs more frequently than other manufacturers' representatives. Most of his new accounts are referred to him by his satisfied customers.

Some incidental aptitudes Fred uses in his work are Number Memory and Finger Dexterity. Number Memory saves him time when he needs information on prices, order numbers, and part numbers. He can remember a lot of numbers instead of going through files to look them up.

His Finger Dexterity comes into play when he demonstrates the fasteners and clips to his clients. Fred does not have Structural Visualization, the three-dimensional thinking aptitude, which means he has to spend extra time talking to engineers to get the technical information he needs. While his job would be easier if he had this spatial-thinking aptitude, his strong Analytical and Diagnostic aptitudes help him compensate—he always asks the right questions to retrieve the facts he needs.

Being a Generalist, he finds it easy to deal with most people. His introverted nature is not as much of a handicap as it would be in sales jobs that required the constant recruiting of new customers and/or the promotion of less practical products.

If *you* are a Diplomat contemplating a sales-oriented job, try to find one that allows you to function as a consultant. Ask yourself these questions about the sales position: Does the job require a rather aggressive personality? Does it require you to create a need in the mind of the customer? Does it require mostly cold calls? Does it require the establishment of many new accounts?

If your answer is "Yes" to most of these questions, your aptitudes as a Diplomat will work *against* you. Just because such a sales job is available to you doesn't mean that it is the *right* one for you, an unfortunate lesson many Diplomats must learn the proverbial hard way.

So You Don't Want To Be A Star

Diplomats must also avoid *any* position with a company that functions on the "star system"—rewarding individuals who stand out, those with razzle-dazzle and a penchant for promoting themselves, and placing low priority on team work and smooth interpersonal transactions.

To motivate its employees, these companies create an environment where competition among peers spawns a survival-of-the-fittest attitude. Stars are those who thrive, often by selling themselves in the political arena.

One well-known brokerage company became notorious for its heartless version of the star system. At the end of each week, a list of all company stockbrokers and their respective sales volume was posted. The two hapless individuals at the bottom of the list were out of a job.

Although Diplomats handle routine company politics quite adeptly, the star system is a problem for them. As mediators in the business world, Diplomats work best in the background. Taking center stage and basking in the adulation of an audience are contrary to the natural tendencies of typical Diplomats.

Don't Rock The Boat

Diplomats with strong Diagnostic ability should also avoid any company with an entrenched bureaucracy. Their critical thinking aptitude quickly gives them a keen awareness of what is wrong or what *could* go wrong—a worthwhile aptitude when your company is interested in change, disastrous when Status Quo is God.

When a company prefers to remain "in the dark" about problems or encourages tradition over change, it is not helpful to perceive what is wrong. If anything, your perceptive ability will just make you and everyone around you miserable.

A number of old, established companies have bureaucracies that rival those of the Federal government. Policies are written in granite, and the large number of employees makes reaction to all but the most severe problems unlikely. Diplomats are regarded as trouble-makers when they voice their concerns about inefficiency or other problems inside such companies.

Ironically, Diplomats show great resourcefulness in finding loopholes in the policy manual and in bending rules to meet a need. If the machinery of the corporate bureaucracy has solidified into a permanent obstacle, however, Diplomats quickly reach the limits of their patience.

Mountains or Mole Hills

The ability of Diplomats to see what is wrong has some other negative implications. When there are no real problems to solve, they either make up some problems or blow minor problems out of proportion. Matters that do not deserve much time and attention suddenly take on great importance, and more significant work is neglected because it is simply not as interesting to the Diplomat.

One office manager with extremely strong Diagnostic and Analytical aptitudes suffered from the lack of an outlet for his problem-solving ability. He was in charge of a regional office for a large restaurant chain, where little was wrong with the way things were being done.

So our Diplomat concentrated on the little problems. He had a 30-minute conference in his office with an employee who was late...once in two years. A misplaced document led to the creation of an elaborate routing procedure for incoming papers. Previously happy and productive employees rebelled.

The restaurant chain reacted by sending the office manager to a location with *real* problems, anticipating that he would get himself into enough trouble to get fired for cause. To the amazement of his superiors, he found ways to correct many of the problems and reorganized the office into a model of efficiency.

Realizing what his true talent was, the company made a habit of regularly sending him to the worst trouble spots. It was suddenly his job to spot problems that mattered, which gave him no reason or time to exaggerate those that didn't.

Overreaction to minor problems can affect Diplomats in another way if they suffer from low self-esteem. Even constructive criticism that seems incidental to someone else has a threatening face to this type of person. Anyone with a poor self-image takes criticism to heart, but the Diplomat with such a problem reads more between the lines than is there.

Diplomats are much more sensitive than most of us when they gauge what other people think or feel. They can easily transform this sensitivity into a kind of paranoia that makes them see themselves as unsatisfactory no matter *how* well they perform their jobs.

Author's Note: Any person whose lack of self-confidence is debilitating should seek professional help. It is doubly important for the Diplomat to seek the services of a psychologist, psychotherapist, or psychiatrist when encountering this type of problem. The critical thinking aptitudes of the Diplomat reinforce negative thinking and quickly turn it into a self-defeating habit.

I Need It Yesterday!

Diplomats should not get themselves into positions requiring instant decisions. A manager in a fast-paced environment frequently shoots from the hip when making decisions. Those with the requisite aptitudes revel in such a world. With no time to weigh the pros and cons, Diplomats in this kind of management position experience a great deal of frustration. Either they feel an unusual amount of conflict in their own minds or postpone any decision until they can accumulate more information.

Subordinates do not characterize these managers as people "highly talented in Diagnostic aptitude."

They're simply called indecisive.

Diplomat Business Careers

Arbitrator

Artist's manager 191.117-010

Athlete manager 153.117-014

Auditor 160.162-014

Bank examiner 160.162-014

Bankruptcy lawyer

Benefits manager 166.167-018

Bonding agent 186.267-010

Booking manager 191.117-014

Business manager or agent (amusement and recreation) 191.117-018

Business writer 131.067-046

Buyer 162.157-018

Casting director (motion pictures; radio and television) 159.267-010

Claim adjuster 241.217-010

Compensation manager 166.167-022

Conciliator 169.207-010

Consumer affairs advisor

Contract administrator 162.117-014

Controller 186.117-014

Corporate communications director

Corporate counsel 110.117-022

Corporate real estate manager

Corporate travel manager

Credit reporter or investigator 241.267-030

Customer complaint service supervisor 241.137-014

Customer services manager 187.167-082

Dealer compliance representative 168.267-026

Detective 376.367-014

Education and training manager 166.167-026

Employee assistance program director

Employee relations representative

Employee services manager 166.117-014

Employee training and development director

Employee welfare manager 166.117-014

Employment interviewer 166.267-010

Employment manager 166.167-030

Estate planner 186.167-010

Field representative 163.267-010

Financial planning consultant

Foreign languages and cultures advisor

Fraud investigator 376.267-014

Government relations advisor

Hospital administrator 187.117-010

Hospital insurance representative 166.267-014

Hotel front office manager 187.167-110

House officer (hotel and restaurant) 376.367-018

Import-export agent 184.117-022

Industrial or organizational psychologist 045.107-030

Industrial relations director 166.117-010

Internal auditor 160.167-034

Internal security manager 376.137-010

International affairs advisor

Issues manager

Labor relations manager 166.167-034

Labor union business representative 187.167-018

Lease buyer (mining and quarrying; petroleum production) 191.117-030

Letter of credit negotiator 186.117-050

Loan officer 186.267-018

Location manager (motion picture; radio and television broadcasting) 191.167-018

Marketing research director

Media buyer

Merchandise manager 185.167-034

Organization and management development director

Overseas branch manager

Personnel or human resources manager 166.117-018

Personnel psychologist

Personnel services manager 166.167-018

Port purser (water transportation) 166.167-038

Process server 249.367-062

Professional sports scout 153.117-018

Purchasing agent 162.157-038

Right of way agent 191.117-046

Risk and insurance manager 186.117-066

Service department manager (wholesale trade) 187.167-142

Service representative 191.167-022

Shopping investigator 376.267-022

Social and political affairs director

Stations relations contact representative (radio and television broadcasting) 184.167-134

Tariff publishing agent 184.167-250

Touring production manager (amusement and recreation) 191.117-038

Traffic manager (radio and television broadcasting) 184.167-090

Trust officer (financial institution) 186.117-074

Undercover operator (retail trade) 376.367-026

Professional and Trade Groups

American Advertising Federation

American Arbitration Association

American Bankers Association

American Bar Association

American College of Healthcare Executives

American Hotel and Motel Association

American Psychological Association

American Society for Personnel Administration

Employment Management Association

Industrial Relations Research Association

Insurance Information Institute

International Association for Financial Planning

International Association of Business
    Communicators
The Institute of Internal Auditors, Inc.
Issues Management Association
Marketing Research Association
National Association of Investigative
    Specialists
National Association of Public Insurance
    Adjusters
National Association of Purchasing
    Management

National Employment Association
National Labor-Management Foundation
National Property Management Association
Property Management Association of
    America
Organizational Development Network
Risk and Insurance Management Society
Society of American Business Editors and
    Writers
Society of Consumer Affairs Professionals in
    Business

Professional Reading

ABA Banker's Weekly
American Import/Export Global Trade
Apparel Industry Magazine
The Arbitration Journal
The Bankers Magazine
Business Credit
Compensation and Benefits Review
The Cornell Hotel and Restaurant
    Management Quarterly
Contract Management
Employee Assistance

Employee Benefit Plan Review
Hotel and Motel Management
Human Resources Management
Journal of Property Management
Landman
Personnel Administrator
Personnel Journal
Personnel Management
Purchasing
Training and Development Journal
Trusts & Estates

GENERALIST *A frame of reference common to most people that facilitates coordination and compromise with others and emphasizes interpersonal skills*

ANALYTICAL *A methodical type of problem-solving ability useful in organizing, coordinating, and planning*

DIAGNOSTIC *An intuitive type of problem-solving ability helpful in investigation and research*

IDEAPHORIA *An imaginative or creative ability useful in generating a rapid flow of ideas and brain-storming*

EXTROVERT *An outgoing, sociable, somewhat impulsive personality*

Weak Reinforcing
Aptitudes

STRUCTURAL VISUALIZATION *The ability to visualize structures in three dimensions*

Five

The Communicators

Kate is the recruiting coordinator for a prestigious law firm in Chicago. Her responsibilities include inviting appropriate law students to participate in summer internships and prospective graduates to visit the firm for interviews. Once an interview is scheduled, Kate must make all travel and hotel arrangements and organize cultural outings and social gatherings to help the potential recruits and the members of the firm size each other up.

Snafus arise often enough to challenge Kate's strong Ideaphoria and Analytical aptitudes. One summer a few years ago, a young lawyer's reluctance to accept a position with the firm was traced to her husband's fear of not being able to find a suitable job in Chicago, more than a thousand miles from their then-home.

The firm's partners agreed that the woman's intelligence and personality made it worthwhile to put extra effort into her recruitment, but they did not know how to allay her husband's fear.

Kate tackled the problem by researching the husband's education and experience, then formulating a list of potential employers and contacts in Chicago. She added comments about particular companies on the list if they were planning expansions, adding new departments, or growing at an unusually fast rate.

After a brainstorming session with Kate helped identify some of the real opportunities available, the newly-secure husband enthusiastically supported his wife's decision to join the law firm.

Kate is a Communicator—an individual who combines the spontaneity of the Persuader with the conflict-resolution capabilities of the Diplomat. The hallmark of Communicators is their skill at digesting a tremendous volume of information and disseminating it in a clear and concise fashion.

A brief survey of Kate's aptitude profile reveals the hybrid nature of a typical Communicator. Like the Diplomat, her Diagnostic ability enabled her to analyze the couple's dilemma and present practical, workable alternatives. Like the Persuader, she then "sold" them on the idea of accepting the firm's offer.

Her job has enough variety to satisfy her strong Ideaphoria—she has no set office hours and is frequently out of the office. It often requires quick thinking to resolve various obstacles that crop up during the interview process. Her work has none of the routine and repetition so deadly to the person with strong Ideaphoria.

Kate's Analytical aptitude—her organizational skill—is an asset, too. She must coordinate the entire interview process from the social calendar to the various meetings with partners. Following the recruiting trip, Kate keeps track of the status of each young lawyer the firm wants to hire.

Often Kate establishes enough rapport with the recruits to learn of their concerns as they consider employment with the firm. Her liaison role between the firm and the recruits is integral to the eventual decisions by both parties.

Kate, an extroverted Generalist, operates on a "wave length" common to most people—a quality that enhances her ability to communicate. Her persuasive personality is suited to her career when tempered by a less aggressive approach.

Focusing on details for long periods of time is rather tedious for her, so she arranges to complete her paperwork in a number of short time periods—a solution for *any* Extrovert with a low tolerance for paperwork.

A Little This, A Little That

Communicators function well in roles that simultaneously encourage both their Extrovert nature *and* their Diagnostic ability. They thrive on the people contact the Diplomat avoids and relish the problem solving the Persuader dismisses.

The biggest mistake a Communicator can make is landing a job that relies on only *one* of these abilities, neglecting his need for a position that satisfies *both* sides of her nature.

Ken made that mistake. Corporate finance seemed like the logical place for him after he completed an MBA program. After interviewing with several blue chip firms, he accepted an offer from an old, established computer company and went to work in capital budgeting and financial analysis.

Only a few months into his new job, Ken began to wonder what it was about financial analysis that he had enjoyed so much as a graduate student—because what*ever* "it" was, it was conspicuously absent in *this* job!

He spent most of his time gathering information, computing figures, and doing spreadsheets, none of which he found particularly satisfying. When he noticed that other employees who had started in his position three or four years earlier were still doing much the same sort of work, he got really worried.

After thoroughly analyzing his aptitudes Ken concluded that he missed active, face-to-face communicating.

Being a financial wizard held no psychological reward for him if he could not use his interpersonal skills. Ken considered leaving finance altogether, because he felt it involved too much number crunching.

But after a lot of research, he stayed in finance, albeit a different branch.

As Ken discussed his problems with a friend in the industry, he learned that the entry-level position in investment banking was much less structured than his current job. Analyzing a client company's financial situation for a possible merger, for the sale of stock, or for other financial transactions comprised much of the work.

Entry-level associates could look forward to meetings with clients in a reasonably short period of time—the key element missing in his present job.

After six weeks of interviews with various investment banking concerns, Ken launched his new career. This is what he says about his new job:

> It's fascinating! These people have superb minds, and they're good at selling their ideas. I think I'm that way, too. I'm spending about seventy hours a week doing this job, and I love it! I can see that I'll be traveling quite a bit before too long, but that's okay. I belong here. I know finance, and I know I can influence people. Eventually I can be creative in investment banking.

Ken's choice of investment banking was based on his interests, background, and a thorough evaluation of where his aptitude profile fit. The interesting fact about Ken is that he was able to use his aptitude profile to narrow his options.

Eliminated on this basis were positions in inventory manage-ment, tax accounting, and cash management. Ken felt that none of these three areas would allow him to capitalize on his ability to present ideas in an exciting way and be innovative in his work—factors that should be weighed heavily by *any* Communicator making a career decision.

Beware Management

If you are a Communicator working for a large corporation, be wary of lusting for the top levels of middle management. The same aptitude profile that made you a creative genius and consummate diplomat on the way up will make you look foolish the closer to the top you get.

Sheila, a public relations practitioner, learned this lesson the hard way. A national, for-profit hospital corporation hired her to do community relations work in a large metropolitan area. The company had three hospitals in a 70-mile radius. Sheila developed programs for all three.

Sheila's duties included giving speeches about health topics to various groups and overseeing the publication of monthly bulletins distributed to physicians and neighborhoods served by the hospitals. When a tornado struck the area, she held the press conferences at the three hospitals to give information on the number of casualties and the way the hospitals were handling the crisis. Her exposure to the public during the press conferences led to her appearance on local television talk shows and a newspaper article which prominently displayed her picture.

Her job was a dream until the company had a major management shake-up and many of its hospitals were assigned different administrators. Despite her lack of training and ignorance of accounting and financial procedures, the headquarters people asked Sheila to assume management responsibilities at one of the three hospitals in her area.

Their logic was that her dynamic public image would help the hospital's financial picture and that a person of Sheila's intelligence could learn the finance necessary to this position. Whatever she didn't learn could be filled in by her subordinates.

Sheila's fatal mistake was *accepting* the job, thinking more money and prestige were prioities.

Sheila's role changed drastically. She still functioned as a spokesperson for the hospital on special occasions, but she spent most of her days doing administrative work.

Controlling costs demanded most of her time. She was dismayed to discover how boring cost control, inventory management, and budgeting really were.

Sheila's knack for creative problem solving left the impression that her solutions were only fluff, leaving conflicts between doctors and administrative staff unresolved. When subordinates in administration and the medical staff began to joke about the dingbat celebrity who was supposed to be running the hospital, Sheila realized her blunder:

> I knew I was doing a poor job. I knew that I could learn to do the job well. But I also knew that I would never *enjoy* it. When I was doing public relations for the hospitals, I had fun. There was always something different to work on.
>
> As an administrator, I had the same problems coming up month after month. I had a talk with myself and decided to move on. I'm now with a public relations agency. I left the hospital before things really went to pot, so my reputation was intact when I went job hunting. I had to take a salary cut, but I am having fun doing work that I am good at. Now my ideas are clever and fresh, not dumb and naive.

Communicators in middle management roles should heed Sheila's hard-won lesson: Your Ideaphoria may be severely frustrated as your administrative duties increase, leaving you hanging onto a corporate ladder...going nowhere.

"Keep It Spicy, Please"

Variety is a key element in any Communicator's job satisfaction. The administrative jobs typical of large, tradition-laden companies offer little outlet for the primary Communicator aptitudes. Smaller companies are usually more dynamic and require each employee to perform a greater variety of tasks—providing the diversity not found in most middle management positions.

Political Land Mines

For the accomplished Communicator, political waters can be navigated with relative ease—it is not unusual for them to be labeled "smooth talkers." Considering the political nature of most organizations, this talent comes in handy.

However, it can backfire when an insecure superior feels threatened. The boss then is likely to plant some landmines for the hapless Communicator—misinformation, unbearable work assignments, projects that are sure-fire losers, etc. Even the most clever Communicator can be trapped in a "no win" situation if an insecure boss continually sets him up to fail.

Not considering the boss's sensitivities is the mistake Megan made in a management job with a greeting card company. The founder of the company, a man in his forties, ran the company. He hired Megan to be the second-in-command because the company had doubled in size in a single year, and he felt he needed managerial help.

Megan knew how this kind of business operated, and she had some ideas on creating some employee-oriented programs. She wanted to have her own company someday, and this position would give her an excellent chance to run a company without having to personally pay for every mistake.

After only a few months, Megan's effectiveness was apparent. Several times each week, employees would pull her aside to make suggestions or unload frustrations. She began to make changes and implement new solutions when she thought the employees had the right ideas or justified complaints. She developed a feel for what was going on in the company.

Megan's boss had very little to say when she brought him up to date on her work—he was much more "at home" with the financial end of the business. This seeming indifference moved Megan to stop reporting as much detail and just present the facts necessary to brief him on the week's activity.

Megan had restructured some of the production workers' time so they could meet as a group once a week to iron out any problems. The boss's apathy became insecurity when he overheard two employees discussing these changes.

In addition to mentioning how much better everyone got along now, they expressed admiration for Megan. One said, "I never thought a woman should be in charge of things, but that gal's okay. You know she's the boss, but she doesn't cram it down your throat. She doesn't take any flak off anybody, but she can joke around with us, too."

The boss's insecurity translated into a perception that Megan was really the one running the company. She had no input in the financial realm, but employee loyalty and efficient operation of the company centered on her, not him. This perception threatened his position, since, unknown to Megan, he owned only 30 percent of the stock in the company he'd founded. He feared that the board of directors might decide that he had served his purpose and replace him with Megan. The whole idea made him mad.

He was the one who started the company. It wouldn't exist if it hadn't been for him. And now because of this young upstart woman they might try to get rid of him. Megan had an uncanny knack for winning people over. If she spent too much time around board members or other big stockholders, they would be convinced of her ability to take over his job. They didn't know too much about her now, so all he'd have to do is tell her that he did not think he could work with her.

And that's exactly what he told her when he fired her that afternoon.

Megan never saw her demise coming. She knew that some other people had stock in the company, but her boss was the founder and, in *her* perception, in control. Megan's mindset precluded any thoughts about her boss's vulnerability.

As a Communicator, Megan had achieved tremendous success with the employees, but failed to appease her insecure boss. Communicators in similar situations need to maintain their efforts to establish loyalty and trust with superiors, convincing the boss that what is good for *you* is ultimately good for *him*—advice Megan would have benefitted from, if only she had known.

If you are a Communicator, do not underestimate the fact that your abilities may pose a threat to those who have the power to affect your progress. In such circumstances, your political skill will be challenged as you try to alleviate the fear of those above you. Your survival will be contingent on your finesse. If you're not up to it, begin seeking a transfer or other employment opportunities...before you have to.

Communicator Business Careers

Advance agent 191.167-010

Advertising account executive

Advertising agency manager 164.117-014

Advertising art director 141.031-010

Advertising copy writer 131.067-014

Advertising creative director 141.067-010

Advertising manager 164.117-010

Advertising sales representative 254.357-014

Area development manager 184.117-030

Artist and repertoire manager 159.167-010

Association executive 189.117-010

Brand or group manager

Brokerage office manager 186.117-034

College relations manager

Communications consultant 253.157-010

Contestant coordinator (radio and television broadcasting) 166.167-010

Convention manager 187.167-078

Convention planner

Crisis manager

Cruise director 352.167-010

Demonstrator 297.354-010

Dental and medical equipment and supplies sales representative (wholesale trade) 276.257-010

Direct marketing manager

Director of community affairs

Director of government relations

Director of investor relations

Director of press and public relations

District, regional, or national sales manager 187.167-138

Education and training developer

Employee publications writer

Exhibit-display representative 297.367-010

Export manager 163.117-014

Fashion coordinator 185.157-010

Financial planning consultant

Graphic art sales representative 254.251-010

Hotel manager 187.117-038

Hotel marketing director

Hotel services sales representative 259.157-014

Investment banker

Literary agent 191.117-034

Loan counselor 186.267-014

Manufacturers' representative (wholesale trade) 279.157-010

Marketing director for arts organization

Meeting planner

Membership director 189.167-026

Motion picture director 159.067-010

Motion picture producer 187.167-174

News director (radio and television broadcasting) 184.167-014

Passenger service representative 359.677-022

Pharmaceutical detailer 262.157-010

Placer (insurance) 239.267-010

Press agent

Printing sales representative 254.357-018

Private label manager

Product manager

Promotion manager 163.117-018

Psychological tests and industrial relations sales agent 251.357-018

Public information officer 165.067-010

Public relations representative 165.067-010

Public service director (radio and television broadcasting) 184.117-010

Publicist

Publisher

Radio and television time sales representative 259.357-018

Radio director 159.167-014

Radio or television producer 159.117-010

Radio or television station manager 184.117-062

Recreation supervisor 187.137-010

Recruiting coordinator for law, accounting, or other large professional firm

Retail store manager 185.167-046

Sales manager 163.167-018

Social director 352.167-010

Special events planner

Speech writer 131.067-046

Sports director (radio and television broadcasting) 184.167-034

Surplus sales officer 163.167-026

Talent agent 191.117-010

Television director 159.067-014

Trade show planner

Trade show representative

Training representative 166.227-010

Wedding consultant 299.357-018

Professional and Trade Groups

Academy of Motion Picture Arts and Sciences

Academy of Television Arts and Sciences

American Advertising Federation

American Association of Advertising Agencies

American Marketing Association

American Society for Personnel Administration

American Society for Training and Development

American Society of Association Executives

American Women in Radio and Television

Association of Bridal Consultants

Association of Sales Administration Managers

Association of Talent Agents

Broadcast Promotion and Marketing Executives

Club Managers Association of America

Hotel Sales and Marketing International

International Association for Financial Planning

International Association of Business Communicators

Manufacturers' Representatives of America

Marketing Communications Executives International

Meeting Planners International

National Association of Performing Arts Managers and Agents

National Investor Relations Institute

National Retail Merchants Associations

Professional Arts Management Institute

Promotional Marketing Association of
America
Public Relations Society of America

Securities Industry Association
Society of Authors' Representatives
Women in Advertising and Marketing

Professional Reading

Advertising Age
Adweek
Agency Sales Magazine
American Import/Export Global Trade
Business Marketing
Chain Store Age Executive
Communication Arts
The Cornell Hotel and Restaurant
Administration Quarterly
Discount Merchandiser
Hotel and Motel Management
Investment Dealer's Digest
Journal of Advertising Research

Journal of Marketing
Marketing and Media Decisions
Marketing Communications
PR News
Public Relations Quarterly
Sales and Marketing Management
The Sporting Goods Dealer
Sports Marketing News
Stores
Successful Meetings
Television/Radio Age
Training and Development Journal

GENERALIST *A frame of reference common to most people that facilitates coordination and compromise with others and emphasizes interpersonal skills*

ANALYTICAL *A methodical type of problem-solving ability useful in organizing, coordinating, and planning*

DIAGNOSTIC *An intuitive type of problem-solving ability helpful in investigation and research*

PERCEPTUAL SPEED *The ability to perform computational and clerical work quickly and accurately*

STRUCTURAL VISUALIZATION *The ability to visualize structures in three dimensions*

Weak Reinforcing
Aptitudes

IDEAPHORIA *An imaginative or creative ability useful in generating a rapid flow of ideas and brain-storming*

Six

The Shirt-Sleeves Managers

Pete exemplifies the Shirt-Sleeves Manager, an individual who enjoys getting his hands dirty as he manages. As the production manager for a medium-size plastics fabrication business, he handles jobs of all kinds and sizes, coordinating the demands of large national department store accounts and the intricacies of numerous custom orders.

Typical of Shirt-Sleeves Managers, Pete spends at least half his time on the production floor, checking the progress of each job and consulting with the production workers and line supervisors when machinery malfunctions.

His contact with subordinates enables Pete to spot morale problems before they fester. His close involvement with the equipment and the operators prevents major breakdowns in the fabrication process, keeping production on schedule.

Organizing, planning, solving problems, working with people, and keeping close watch on production or paperwork processes should all be part of the Shirt-Sleeves Manager's job, since he or she ideally balances the "doing" part of the job with the managing part.

Shirt-Sleeves Managers share many traits with the Diplomats discussed in Chapter 4. As Generalists, both types find themselves on the same "wave length" as most other people. Strong in the Analytical and/or Diagnostic aptitudes, they surmise the motives of others with uncommon ease.

What differentiates the Shirt-Sleeves Managers from the Diplomats is their strong aptitude for performing tasks requiring three-dimensional thinking (Structural Visualization) or those requiring computational and clerical speed and accuracy (Perceptual Speed), both of which are "doing" rather than "thinking" aptitudes.

Pete perfectly illustrates this distinction as he coordinates the many phases of the production process. To schedule production runs efficiently, he considers the type of equipment to be used and the processes required for the completion of each phase. This series of tasks would be impossible for him without his strong Structural Visualization. He must decide which machinery to use, which employees would perform best on each, even which will best fulfill the job specs. You might say Pete is the force behind the process.

These "doing" aptitudes put Shirt-Sleeves Managers in close touch with the actual work being performed. Instead of focusing primarily on the "people problems" in a business, as Diplomats do, Shirt-Sleeves Managers have a hand in making sure that reports are done on time, production schedules met, and that the company operates efficiently in other ways. He rolls up his shirt-sleeves to get the job done.

No Specialists Allowed

Another factor in the typical Shirt-Sleeves Manager's success is his Generalist frame of reference and Ambivert personality. Like Pete, most Shirt-Sleeves Managers are in roles that require extensive interaction with co-workers—this may be overseeing a crew or consulting with engineers about custom orders. Pete shares a common point of view with those he oversees, which allows him to perceive morale problems and place workers on machines where they feel most comfortable.

If Pete were a Specialist or an Introvert, his lack of interpersonal skills would undermine his effectiveness as a manager. If you are a Specialist or an Introvert who prefers working alone, then you would be much better suited to the Gnome profile described in the next chapter.

Do You Thrive On Stress?

Pete thrives on stress—he actually *enjoys* the pressure that accompanies the deadlines and time constraints that are his responsibility to meet. Other people with Pete's aptitudes prefer jobs that require less juggling of their time and priorities.

This trait has nothing to do with aptitudes, but it is an important component of job satisfaction—and one to be reckoned with before you accept a position that involves stringent time pressures.

If you are a Shirt-Sleeves Manager but hate being "under the gun" of an impending deadline, you would be well-advised to seek a position that seldom requires adjusting to last-minute surprises.

Anne's job title—systems analyst—might not *say* "manager," but she does what Shirt-Sleeves Managers in many companies do. She puts herself in the midst of the action, pays attention to the details of how everything is done, but doesn't let them cloud her perception of the overall situation.

Anne can put things into logical order so that both computers and people can deal with the information they need. She organizes the work of the programmers and manages projects to their conclusions.

Anne might have experienced more difficulty if she had begun her career in the way most systems analysts do—as a computer programmer. The programming position fits the Introvert. Anne is more socially oriented and would have found that working several years as a programmer was not people-oriented enough. Her accounting background qualified her for the analyst's position right away.

Starting at the systems analyst level allowed Anne to continue in a field that involved her with people as well as information systems problems. Her job is much more general than those of most accountants, too. She does deal with accounting information in many of her projects, but those projects almost always involve broader problems.

Anne used her accounting degree and computer courses to get the systems analyst position. Business degrees in management science or information systems, systems analysis, and operations research are suitable for jobs similar to Anne's. Courses in these fields take a quantitative approach to business problems and can lead to consulting or management positions like Anne's.

These jobs might not involve using Structural Visualization, but they do involve using Analytical and Perceptual Speed aptitudes. Extroverts enjoy the jobs that put them into direct contact with clients and that allow them to train people who must use the newly-designed system.

When New Ideas Get In The Way

Shirt-Sleeves Managers benefit from a particular weak aptitude, one that contributes as much to their success as their strengths. The significance of weak Ideaphoria aptitude to the Shirt-Sleeves Manager lies in the need for consistency in the production process.

Most production work necessitates slow change, allowing workers the time to learn the most efficient ways to accomplish specific tasks. Managers that are always generating a new idea impede production, as their subordinates need to focus on implementing change rather than expediting the work to be done.

Even though she has strong Ideaphoria, Marie was unbelievably efficient in her work, not making the absent-minded mistakes typical of such people. Her responsibilities included keeping track of when and where meeting and conference rooms were being used and knowing who was to participate in which meetings.

As long as Marie spent only half her working day on meetings, both she and her boss were happy. Marie got to spend the other half of the day writing news releases and contributing to brainstorming sessions when fresh ideas were needed for trade shows or other events. These activities provided outlets for her Ideaphoria aptitude.

Then Marie's job changed. The company decided it would be logical to expand Marie's meetings and facilities coordinating job duties. This change took Marie out of the public relations department and into the operations department. The time she had spent doing pubic relations work was now devoted to tracking down schedule conflicts and trying to computerize the meetings schedule, the facility availability, and the participants' schedules. Now Marie's Ideaphoria had no outlets.

The problem with Marie's expanded job was that it called for a consistent, no-nonsense approach and a great deal of concentration on noncreative tasks. Marie's Ideaphoria was better suited to an imaginative approach. She could perform well when *half* her day demanded concentrated effort in an unimaginative job, but her expanded job required a full eight hours of noncreative work, and the amount of detail increased exponentially. This caused Marie to daydream frequently. Her performance was abysmal.

Marie's aptitude profile is actually closer to that of the Communicators described in Chapter 5. Eventually she joined a public relations firm that does extensive lobbying. Now she creates brochures and other pieces of public information, writes speeches, and has become quite successful. Her only regret is that she did not recognize the difference between Shirt-Sleeves Managers and Communicators sooner.

No College Degree Required

Unlike some management positions within the business sector, many production and manufacturing managers "cut their teeth" in entry-level roles, learning the jobs they will eventually oversee. Shirt-Sleeves Managers often begin their careers in blue collar positions where on-the-job training gives them the necessary foundation for a management role. Many who have succeeded started in hourly positions and were promoted to foremen or line supervisor.

Those with college degrees are more likely to become plant managers with more significant responsibilities. Some colleges and universities offer degrees in such specific fields as construction management and printing operations management. These degree programs combine business courses with technical courses peculiar to the field, and they are excellent preparation for the Shirt-Sleeves Manager.

Education or experience in technical fields like engineering or in specialized business fields like accounting or systems analysis provides a springboard for the Shirt-Sleeves Manager, but it cannot assure management success. If the Shirt-Sleeves Manager neglects to develop the interpersonal skills of effective managers, he will fail.

For the typical Shirt-Sleeves Manager, this transition from laborer to supervisor can result in a career-threatening dilemma. Their knack for quickly resolving a glitch often makes them impatient with subordinates who are slower.

Real difficulties arise when Shirt-Sleeves Managers fail to realize that their natural "problem solving" and "doing" aptitudes do not exist in everyone—they catch on to things faster than most people and frequently assume that these things should be apparent to everyone.

As a result, the Shirt-Sleeves Manager sometimes fails to be explicit when directing subordinates or giving instruction. He loses patience with diligent workers who require more time to learn a new task or assimilate a change in procedure. Such Shirt-Sleeves Managers are easily frustrated when they think an employee is taking too much time to complete a form, make calculations, or read a blueprint.

If you are a Shirt-Sleeves Manager and responsible for keeping subordinates motivated, be aware that your aptitudes are *not* common to everyone.

Do *not* assume that your subordinates see what is "obvious" to you.

Make *sure* that they do, and proceed from there.

The time you spend explaining things will result in fewer misunderstandings and mistakes.

Also be aware that many subordinates cannot complete certain tasks as quickly as you can. Their lack of speed might not reflect a lack of motivation, merely the lack of a particular aptitude.

As a manager, a major part of your success depends on your subordinates. Allocate enough time to them so that you can communicate with a patient and accepting attitude. Recognize their limitations so that you can plan and schedule their work appropriately.

Seminars and classroom courses in organizational development and management theory can provide some understanding of the human problems in management. The neophyte Shirt-Sleeves Manager might find such courses very helpful.

Paul, a land site coordinator for a real estate developer, learned this management lesson the hard way—because of his bullish attitude, he went through five assistants in one year.

Paul had received almost no training for his job. His father had been a building and construction contractor, so he grew up knowing a lot about the business from summer jobs with his father's company and casual conversations with his father. He went to work for a real estate developer shortly after dropping out of college during his sophomore year.

The first time he went to the court house to find out who owned a certain block of land, he asked a secretary there how the records were organized and figured out how to get the information he needed. Paul's strong Analytical and Diagnostic aptitudes made this challenge a fairly easy one for him.

When he hired an assistant a few years later, Paul assumed that the assistant would learn the ropes at the court house as easily as he had. After foundering for a month or two, the assistant quit, and Paul hired another one.

The story repeated itself five times before Paul realized that the problem was not an unfortunate series of stupid assistants, but his own neglect in training and managing them. He spent more time with the sixth assistant and developed a valuable subor-dinate.

All The Blame. No Credit!

Another potential problem for Shirt-Sleeves Managers exists when companies hold line positions in low regard. Many Shirt-Sleeves Managers are in low-profile roles that involve facilitating the production of goods or the flow of paper. If a company rewards its sales force or its acquisitions team at the expense of the people who keep things running efficiently, Shirt-Sleeves Managers fare poorly.

In these companies, Shirt-Sleeves Managers are taken for granted...usually until an ordinarily smooth operation develops a delay or another problem. Then *they* get blamed!

Today's trend toward cutting costs, streamlining pro-duction, and developing just-in-time inventory systems promises greater rewards for Shirt-Sleeves Managers. Some people see this trend as the last frontier in improving the profitability of business. Shirt-Sleeves Managers who develop their managerial skills along with their ability for solving problems and getting things done will be on the leading edge of this frontier.

Shirt-Sleeves Manager Business Careers

Accounting clerks supervisor 216.132-010

Accounts receivable manager

Airport manager 184.117-026

Auction assistant 294.667-010

Automotive services manager 184.117-034

Building and construction contractor 182.167-010

Business librarian 100.167-026

Cargo and ramp services manager (air transportation) 184.167-058

Cash management officer

Chief business programmer 020.167-018

Chief dietitian 077.117-010

Chief information officer

Chief pilot 196.167-010

Chief planner 012.165-050

Christmas tree farm manager 180.117-010

Construction superintendent 182.167-026

Credit card operations manager 186.167-022

Customer technical services manager 189.117-018

Customs house broker 186.117-018

Dairy farm manager 180.167-026

Dealer accounts credit officer 161.267-014

Director of employment research and planning 050.117-010

Display manager 142.031-014

Distribution manager

Distribution superintendent (light, heat, and power) 184.167-154

Distribution warehouse manager 185.167-018

Electronic data processing manager 169.167-030

Environmental research project manager 029.167-014

Estimator 160.267-018

Executive chef 187.161-010

Executive housekeeper (hotel and restaurant; medical services) 187.167-046

Facilities manager

Facilities planner 019.261-018

Factory manager 183.117-014

Field contractor 162.117-022

Field service manager

Fish hatchery manager 180.167-030

Flight reservations manager 184.167-070

Food processing plant manager 183.167-026

Food service manager 187.167-106

Forest nursery supervisor 451.137-010

Forms analysis manager 161.167-014

Game breeding farm manager 180.167-034

Game preserve manager 180.167-038

General manager (farm) 180.167-018

Harvest contractor 409.117-010

Hazard control manager

Horticultural specialty farming supervisor 405.131-010

Industrial organization manager 189.117-022

International banking officer 186.167-014

Inventory manager

Land development manager 186.117-042

Land leases and rentals manager (petroleum production) 186.167-038

Law firm manager

Leased machinery and equipment service supervisor 183.167-030

Livestock yard supervisor 410.134-010

Logistics manager

Maintenance superintendent (air transportation) 184.167-174

Mapping supervisor (petroleum production; pipe lines) 018.167-030

Material coordinator 222.167-014

Material expediter 221.367-042

Material scheduler (aircraft and aerospace manufacturing) 012.187-010

Materials manager

Meetings and facilities coordinator

Metallurgical and quality control testing supervisor 011.161-010

Mine superintendent (mining and quarrying) 181.117-014

Nursery manager 180.167-042

Occupational health nursing director 075.117-026

Office planning representative 019.261-018

Oil well services field supervisor 930.131-010

Operations director (radio and television broadcasting) 184.167-018

Operations manager 184.117.050

Operations officer (financial institution) 186.167-050

Pension fund manager

Photogrammetry flight operations director 184.167-026

Physician executive

Planning supervisor 012.165-050

Plant manager 183.117-014

Poultry hatchery manager 180.167-046

Printing shop supervisor 659.130-010

Procurement services manager 162.167-022

Production control supervisor 221.137-018

Production coordinator 221.167-018

Production engineering tooling coordinator (aircraft and aerospace manufacturing) 169.167-054

Production manager 183.117-014

Production planner 012.167-050

Production scheduler 012.165-050

Production superintendent (agriculture) 180.167-058

Project director 189.117-030

Project engineer 019.167-014

Prop-making supervisor (motion pictures) 962.137-022

Property coordinator (amusement and recreation; radio and television broadcasting) 962.167-018

Property manager (real estate) 186.167-046

Publications production manager 979.131-010

Quality assurance manager

Quality control director 012.167-014

Rate supervisor 214.137-018

Records analysis manager 161.167-018

Records management director 161.117-014

Reports analysis manager 161.167-022

Research and development director 189.117-014

Research director (motion pictures; radio and television broadcasting) 052.167-010

Reserve officer (financial institution; insurance) 186.167-054

Safety manager 012.167-058

Schedule planning manger (air transportation) 184.117-058

Service director 189.167-014

Ship's captain 197.167-010

Shipping and receiving supervisor 222.137-030

Space scheduler or conference center coordinator 238.367-022

Stage manager 159.167-018

Superintendent of generation (light, heat, and power) 184.167-138

Supermarket manager

Supervisor of communications 184.167-230

Technical director (radio and television broadcasting) 962.162-010

Telecommunications manager

Television schedule coordinator 199.387-010

Title supervisor 119.167-018

Traffic manager 184.167-094

Translation director 137.137-010

Transportation superintendent 184.167-226

Transportation director 184.117-014

Travel agency manager 187.167-158

Underwriting clerks supervisor (insurance) 219.132-022

Vendor quality supervisor 012.167-062

Water and sewer systems superintendent 184.161-014

Professional and Trade Groups

Academy of Hazard Control Management

American Association of Airport Executives

American Institutions Food Service Association

American Production and Inventory Control Society

American Society for Quality Control

American Society of Appraisers

American Society of Transportation and Logistics

American Society of Travel Agents

Association for Systems Management

Association of Field Service Managers, International

Association of Records Managers and Administrators

Council of Logistics Management

Data Processing Management Association

National Association of Retail Grocers of the United States

National Property Management Association

Project Management Institute

Society of Real Estate Appraisers— Communications Division

Tele-Communications Association

Professional Reading

The Appraisal Journal

Automation

Building Operating Management

Buildings: The Facilities Construction and Management Magazine

Business Credit

Communications News

Data Communications

Distribution

Dr. Dobb's Journal of Software Tools

Food Processing

Footwear Manufacturing

Health Care Management

Industrial Development and Site Selection Handbook

Industrial Distribution

Institutional Distribution

Journal of Property Management

Journal of Systems Management

Management Science

Restaurant Management

Telephony

Traffic Management for Logistics Managers

SPECIALIST *A unique frame of reference that indicates a subjective outlook and emphasizes personal competence and independent action*

ANALYTICAL *A methodical type of problem-solving ability useful in organizing, coordinating, and planning*

DIAGNOSTIC *An intuitive type of problem-solving ability helpful in investigation and research*

PERCEPTUAL SPEED *The ability to perform computational and clerical work quickly and accurately*

Weak Reinforcing
Aptitudes

IDEAPHORIA *An imaginative or creative ability useful in generating a rapid flow of ideas and brain-storming*

STRUCTURAL VISUALIZATION *The ability to visualize structures in three dimensions*

Seven

The
Gnomes

Stan's boss once described him as a loaded gun—
"very effective, but you *do* have to watch where you point him."

Stan, like most Gnomes, possesses the innate ability to
focus on one particular, narrow subject, study the mountains
of detail associated with it, then consolidate everything into a
thorough grasp of the material.

Such inherent skill has made Stan a very competent
research analyst for a large brokerage firm. He is renowned
for his "leave no stone unturned" approach in his investiga-
tions of various gas and oil concerns. The firm uses his
findings to determine which securities the brokers should
recommend to their clients, which companies are appropriate
takeover targets, and which new companies are good underwriting possibilities.

It's easy to see how Stan uses his aptitudes in his work. Meticulous attention to detail uses his Perceptual Speed. His strong Analytical and Diagnostic aptitudes come into play as he methodically applies his knowledge and looks for clues to problems in the companies he investigates.

He is an introverted Specialist, an ideal personality for the concentrated, uni-directional effort required in his research job. Stan is blessed with Number Memory aptitude, and his brain teems with figures and facts about the oil and gas business. He works single-mindedly to apply this data to the task at hand.

Stan is the best at what he does—he has effectively manipulated his Gnome profile into a very strong and rewarding career.

When Gnomes Fail

Stan's currently unassailable reputation was not achieved without some bumps along the way. Many Specialist Introvert Gnomes like Stan fall prey to the "loaded gun" remark because they fail—often miserably—to hone their "rough edges." Or care about honing them.

Stan's personality has impeded his career at times, usually when he became so focused on thoroughness and accuracy that he failed to perceive the drastic consequences of his findings. Due to a particular lack of tact and discretion in accommodating a rather ticklish political situation, for example, he was forced to resign a research position at a similar firm.

Harry, vice president in the investment banking department, was enthusiastic about a particular oil and gas company. One of his old college buddies had become president the previous year, and the company had increased its oil and gas production by 20 percent since his friend's arrival.

When Harry's friend asked him if his firm would be interested in underwriting a new stock offering, Harry was flattered and ecstatic, already anticipating the hefty bonus and equally-exhilerating rise in stature he'd receive if the offering were successful. He felt that the recent performance of his friend's company would make it an attractive investment. Harry described the company in glowing terms to others in his department, and he eagerly awaited Stan's favorable report to get the ball rolling.

Stan tackled the research assignment with his characteristic fervor. He found some disturbing bits of information right away and delved deeper into the numbers. Days of research evolved into weeks. Finally, Harry dropped into Stan's office to see why the report was taking so long.

"This company is a dog," Stan announced without preamble. "I'll give you all the gory details when I get this report finished."

Harry was completely nonplussed. Stan's brutally honest way of reporting the bad news caught him totally off guard. Worse, when Harry asked for the gist of Stan's findings—he needed to extricate himself from the promotion of his friend's company and the accompanying embarrassment as quickly as possible—Stan brusquely declined. It was simply not his way to release incomplete information, regardless of the supposed need.

Harry's unhappy encounter with Stan soon festered into intense dislike when Stan, with characteristic bluntness, dropped his bomb at a weekly meeting. The company was a very risky investment at best, he calmly stated, and one that could be disastrous over time. Among other unpalatable details, Stan expounded at length about the fact that executive salaries had doubled during the past year.

Stan's findings were indisputable and especially embarrassing to Harry. He had lost face, a development, he convinced himself, that was all Stan's fault. Harry had to explain to his buddy, the oil and gas company president, why his firm had placed such a low value on the stock. It was a difficult thing to discuss without impugning his friend's integrity. Harry's stature at work was in jeopardy also. He had loudly proclaimed the wonders of this oil and gas company and its president; now he had to eat crow.

Harry's associates soon started kidding him about "Swindle Top." Harry put on a good-natured front when his friend's company surfaced as a topic of conversation. But underneath, he was seething and vengeful. He launched an insidious campaign against Stan. Harry never questioned Stan's work or technical competency—he knew Stan was unassailable on those fronts. But Stan's mannerisms, personality, and dress were more easily attacked.

Harry soon found more than enough opportunties to insert casual comments about Stan, comments that festered and took on a life of their own around the company. "Stan's got all the couth of Attila the Hun," Harry would ruefully remark to another vice president. "It's a good thing he's not our ambassador to Russia. We'd have been nuked by now." Or, more venomously: "You ever wonder what planet he came from?" "How can a guy that bright be such a jerk?" "It's not so much what he says as how he says it that makes you wonder about him."

With Harry's help, Stan's boss noticed that Stan did *not* make a big effort to get along with people. Soon other executives began noticing and commenting on Stan's abrupt manner. Stan didn't find it particularly gratifying to play the political game. Like many other introverted Specialists, he believed that his work spoke for itself. It was his job to provide accurate information and objective analyses, and he did just that.

When Stan's boss told him he should try harder to get along with other people, Stan was insulted.

When he was later informed that his continued lack of progress in developing interpersonal skills could lead to his dismissal, Stan seethed with anger but still said nothing.

Finally, when his boss told Stan that he must change or else, Stan resigned.

Avoiding The Precipice

Stan's case is not an isolated instance of a Gnome drowning in political waters. Many Gnomes in the corporate culture relate strikingly similar misfortunes. If you are a Specialist Gnome like Stan, your career survival rests in your recognizing the limitations of your personality and finding situations that compensate for them.

Problems arise when you are required to "wing it" in informal interactions outside your realm of expertise. The compromises and political favors inherent in the corporate ladder-climbing game are *not* second nature to you.

A Gnome functions best in situations that allow him to be an expert or authority. Being a nice guy—one who gets the job done by getting along with everyone—is simply not his strength (or, for that matter, his concern).

It didn't take Stan long to find another full service brokerage firm to employ him. His work activities in his current job are much the same as they were with his previous employer, with one notable exception: The day-to-day situations requiring skillful political and diplomatic moves are handled by his boss, insulating Stan from potentially disastrous encounters with other people. By managing him as the introverted Specialist he is, Stan's boss has allowed him to do exactly what he does best.

Becoming An Expert

The Gnome profits more than any other business person from specialized training. In fact, such training is virtually a requirement: When a Gnome *neglects* to develop an expertise, his career invariably takes a disappointing turn.

Keri, an Introverted Specialist, is a Gnome who failed to acknowledge her need for specialization. Her wayward trek began when she chose to attend a small private college and major in liberal arts. Upon graduation, she accepted an offer from a telecommunications concern that had trained other liberal arts grads for sales positions.

Keri was only partially successful—she sold *herself* on the idea. On the sales personality test administered by the personnel department, she tried her best to answer the questions as (she thought) a successful sales representative would.

The employment interviewer told Keri that the personality test results were inconclusive. Keri did *not* have the ideal sales personality profile, but she didn't have the sure-fire *failure* profile either. The company encouraged hiring women, so Keri was offered a job. She took it.

And she never made it out of the training program. After a week or so of classes similar to her lectures at college, the trainees formed supervised teams for role playing. When Keri played the role of sales representative, she retreated each time the "potential customer" raised an objection.

When the trainer urged Keri to overcome these objections, Keri argued. "How am I supposed to know more about it than the customer? Maybe the customer has no need for a different system."

The trainer replied, "Just be friendly and loosen up a bit. Talk to the prospect about some of the benefits of our systems. Remember all the advantages we discussed in class? You could hit on just the right thing to interest someone."

"That's hard to do when you've got a strong-willed person in front of you," Keri persisted. "It's hard to see how we could help a customer who comes up with some of these reasons not to buy. I think that some people are actually better off without our system. Why should they buy it if they don't need it?"

Keri bailed out after three arduous days of role playing. The classes had become debating sessions with the trainer, and the trainer did not appreciate Keri's effect on the rest of the class. When she told him that she was quitting, he suggested that she think about what she truly liked to do before interviewing for another job...but to definitely avoid sales positions.

Just Before You Leap...

As Keri analyzed herself, she recognized that she had decided against a trainee position as a computer programmer primarily because this would commit her to a specialization. She feared such immediate specialization would limit her career possibilities. Keri soon realized that she actually functioned *best* when she operated on the basis of specialized knowledge and when her work was based on individual effort instead of her ability—or inability—to influence other people.

Gnomes like Keri find specialized training essential to career success. They cannot rely on their personalities to pave the way for them. As we saw in Stan's case, that personality can easily be a drawback! Gnomes who are Specialists can easily antagonize co-workers and customers without even realizing it.

Personal competence, not interpersonal relationships, reinforces the natural bent of the Gnome. A deep knowledge of a specialized area gives the Gnome a way to offset the problems that will inevitably arise from his inadvertent mistakes in handling people.

At the same time, the development of specialized knowledge or skill takes advantage of the introverted Specialist's ability to apply his undivided attention to the task at hand.

Hard Work Works

There are some Gnomes who have succeeded without the full complement of aptitudes for this type of business career. Lacking the Analytical, Diagnostic, or Perceptual Speed aptitude, they simply worked harder than anyone to learn more about their specialties.

Jill is a good example—an introverted Specialist who lacks strong Analytical, Diagnostic *and* Perceptual Speed aptitudes.

Because her parents could not afford college expenses and all the schools that offered her scholarships were too far away from home, Jill got a full-time job as a clerk in the personnel department of a large electronics manufacturing company and took courses at the community college at night.

The job required her to sift through job applications and sort them according to rules dictated by her supervisor. Jill wrote down the specifications her supervisor told her to use when classifying the job applications. Some of the positions in the company required very specific types of degrees or skill combinations.

Certain vacancies in the company needed to be filled quickly, so Jill had to find job applicants who might qualify even though they had applied for different positions. If the company was falling short of its goal for minority employees in certain jobs, for example, Jill was instructed to make finding applicants from minority groups a priority.

Taking the conscientious approach so typical of her, Jill checked and rechecked her list of specifications as she reviewed job applications. When she found that the company had numerous manuals covering its hiring and employment practices, she used them to look up details that confused her. If she was still unsure about a detail, she asked her supervisor for help.

After Jill's first year on the job, her supervisor began asking *her* for information. When Jill didn't know the answers, she persisted until she found them.

Jill earned a associate's degree in business management from the community college. Today she is an expert at the electronics company. She makes sure that it's hiring practices comply with Federal, state and local government regulations and that it meets its goals for employing women and members of racial minorities.

The company pays the tuition for her evening classes at a four-year college, and her boss has promised that it will pay her tuition to law school and full pay for a three-day work week if she decides to attend.

Jill has succeeded by slowly and steadily building up knowledge about a very specific field. She knows more than anyone else in her company about her specialty, despite the fact that she lacks a number of aptitudes seemingly necessary for such a job. She has compensated for her limited aptitudes by working harder and longer than most people and by focusing on the narrowest possible area.

You Can't Fake It

If you are a Gnome, you *must* realize that actual competence is essential to your career success. The business world is littered with breathing beings that slighted this reality and are now pounding the pavement.

Steve is someone who, despite a full complement of analytical and problem-solving aptitudes, assiduously developed the image of an expert without really being one.

As a teenager, Steve realized that he would never succeed by glad-handing and being "Mr. Personality." But he knew he was generally smarter than his friends and even some of his teachers.

Steve majored in history and philosophy in college. They were easy subjects for him, and his college was not an academically demanding one. Most of his tests were discussion and essay. Steve expounded on the events or principles in question with little effort and made it a point to throw in some obscure details to properly impress his professors.

Steve began his descent into self-deception while still in college, falling into the habit of writing term papers at the last minute. Sometimes he invented convincing references to support the thesis of his paper. It was, he reasoned, a necessary evil. After all, time was short, and his actual library research often yielded information more complicated than he had anticipated. His fake information was convincing (and never questioned) because he had developed a reputation for being such a smart fellow.

After graduating, Steve applied to several graduate schools with the idea of acquiring a Ph.D. in economics. His grade point average and Graduate Record Exam scores made him a prime candidate. Two highly regarded schools accepted him.

To the amazement of his friends and the consternation of his parents, Steve chose to enroll in the third-rate economics program at his "backup school."

His public rationale was that this program would allow him more latitude in designing his research and that he could develop his expertise along the lines he thought best.

In reality, Steve knew that he'd simply rather be the top student in an inferior program than one of many bright people at a competitive school. He suspected that he could apply some of the same tactics he had used as an undergraduate and easily get by.

He was right.

Although Steve spent more time gathering data for his research, he still used the insufficient knowledge he gained to guide him to reasonable, if not totally accurate, explanations.

When he did not know the material his professors expected him to, he would simply combine his superficial understanding with some outright fabrications.

Applying himself half the time and bluffing the rest, Steve got his Ph.D. and interviewed for a research position with a think tank of econometric forecasters. He got the research job and looked forward to work that would be much like his graduate school days.

Steve's job disappointed him within a few weeks. He found his work narrowly focused and highly detailed. Unlike the top people in the institute, he spent none of his time theorizing and discussing alternatives to various economic situations.

Instead, his bosses expected him to delve into reams of numerical data about interest rates, money supplies, disposable income, government spending, industrial back orders, and other such arcane information. They wanted summaries, details, and explanations he could give them only after days or weeks of meticulous research and diligent cross-checking.

In his school work, Steve had perfected the art of "guesstimating" data when he encountered complex or contradictory information. His professors had been satisfied with his conceptual grasp of economics, but they had not been meticulous in checking the specific data he used. Steve worked with the assumption that his bosses would be the same. Unfortunately for Steve, his bosses were different.

Sensitive to the common criticism that economists are almost never right in their projections, the bosses, in fact, were fanatical in their demands for accuracy. When frequent discrepancies between Steve's data and that of another researcher became apparent, alarm bells rang. The other researcher proved to have the correct data. Steve could not explain why his information was wrong. How could he tell them he had simply made it up on the basis of what he *thought* was reasonable?

Steve lost confidence in his future as a research economist. He eventually found a teaching post with a small state college in the Southwest.

The irony is that Steve possessed the Gnome's ideal aptitude profile, an excellent one for economics research. His mistake, perhaps rooted in psychological problems, was applying those aptitudes to the *image or appearance* of expertise instead of to the development of the expertise itself.

To be a Gnome in the *real* world of business, you must develop a high degree of *real* competence. Steve's example proves that this precept is true even in economics, a field thought by many to give its experts considerable latitude with the facts.

Keep Your Ideas To Yourself

The Gnome with strong Ideaphoria is a cursed individual, since Ideaphoria interferes with the concentrated focus necessary for success as a Gnome. Erika, an erstwhile computer programmer with strong Ideaphoria, described the dilemma this way:

> I was okay the first hour at work. My mind was fresh, and I could get psyched up to go in there and do it right. Then I'd begin daydreaming. I'd fantasize about writing a recipe book and how you could make photos of what the dish was supposed to look like in various stages of preparation and do the pages in some sort of plastic that you could wipe off.
>
> All this would make me start thinking of ideas for children's books. Then it would be coffee break time. The progress on my computer program wouldn't look too bad because I'd been so fired up for the first hour.
>
> After the morning coffee break, things would get really bad. I'd sit down with every intention of getting fired up again, but after about fifteen minutes, I'd just stare at my stuff and try to convince myself that it wasn't really boring.
>
> Then I'd muse about when I was still in school and about how I loved computer courses back then. That would make me think about the concerts and plays I attended when I was a student and about how much time I spent reading novels and short stories.
>
> After lunch, I'd be so shocked at how little I'd accomplished that I'd *really* get with it until the afternoon coffee break. I knew that if I did enough in those two hours, I could

slough off until quitting time. I think everyone noticed how much better the other programmers were, and that really hurt me. I wanted to be the best, but I just couldn't get into computer programming like I thought I could.

Obviously, Erika's performance was less than stellar. Her Ideaphoria inhibited her concentration, thwarting her efforts as a programmer. Unless she finds an outlet for this aptitude, she is destined to struggle. The Gnome nature does not readily lend itself to Ideaphoria-oriented careers.

Forests, Trees, Branches...

Even Gnomes with the ideal set of aptitudes can fall short of their career ambitions. There are those perfectly suited for their work and experts in their specialized fields who, like experts in many fields outside business, sometimes fail to grasp a comprehensive view of things.

Gnomes preoccupy themselves with their particular tasks, often neglecting to see how these specific tasks fit into the overall scheme of things. Their narrow focus can quickly become a liability.

It's not just that the Gnome cannot see the forest for the trees; he cannot see the tree for the branches.

This tendency to deal with detail to the exclusion of the general picture can be controlled. Simply being aware of this predisposition should help you guard against it. Having an effective manager to fit the work of various specialists into a cohesive pattern would also be beneficial.

Remember Stan, the analyst in the research department at the brokerage firm? His boss described him as a loaded gun, "very effective, but you do have to watch where you point him." That description illustrates the powerful skill or knowledge of the Gnome—"the loaded gun," who functions best in an environment structured to aim his efforts at an appropriate target.

The right boss and organizational structure can mold detail-oriented Gnomes into an effective work force. Stan's second employer provided a more suitable environment for Gnomes than did his first employer, simply by making sure there was a buffer—Stan's boss—between the researchers and other departments.

Final Warnings

From the varied experiences we have considered here, you must realize that Gnomes face a slew of hazards to career success. If you see yourself as a Gnome, you should evaluate your career options according to the following pitfalls that have entrapped other Gnomes:

DO avoid choosing a company that has a poor organizational structure or poor reward system for its specialists.

DO NOT underestimate the necessity of developing competence in a specialized field.

DO work to broaden your horizons to encompass the "big picture."

NEVER seek a career where personality is essential to success.

NEVER, *NEVER* feign an "image" of expertise to cover up your lack of *real* knowledge.

Gnome Business Careers

Abstractor 119.267-010

Accident and sickness insurance underwriter 169.167-058

Account analyst 214.382-010

Actuary 020.167-010

Administrative analyst 090.167-018

Applied statistician 020.067-026

Appraiser 191.287-014

Automobile insurance underwriter 169.167-058

Benefits and compensation analyst

Bond insurance underwriter 169.167-058

Budget accountant 160.167-014

Building inspector 168.267-010

Business programmer 020.162-014

Casualty insurance underwriter 169.167-058

Claim examiner (insurance) 168.267-014

Clerical methods analyst 161.267-010

Commodity industry economist 050.067-010

Compensation insurance underwriter 169.167-058

Contract specialist 162.117-018

Cost accountant 160.167-018

Credit life insurance underwriter 169.167-058

Credit analyst 191.267-014

Economist 050.067-010

Electronic data processing systems analyst 012.167-066

Equal opportunity and affirmative compliance specialist

Financial analyst 020.167-014

Financial economist 050.067-010

Fire insurance underwriter 169.167-058

Food and beverage analyst (hotel and restaurant) 310.267-010

Forms analyst 161.267-018

Freight rate analyst 214.267-010

Group insurance underwriter 169.167-058

Industrial economist 050.067-010

Information scientist 109.067-010

Information system programmer 020.187-010

Insurance attorney 110.117-014

Insurance underwriter 169.167-058

International trade economist 050.067-010

Job analyst 166.267-018

Labor economist 050.067-010

Liability insurance underwriter 169.167-058

Logistics specialist 019.167-010

Management analyst 161.167-010

Management information systems specialist

Marine insurance underwriter 169.167-058

Market research analyst 050.067-014

Mathematician 020.167-014

Methods and procedures analyst 012.167-066

Money market analyst

Multiple line insurance underwriter 169.167-058

Operations research analyst 020.067-018

Parts cataloger 229.267-010

Patent lawyer 110.117-026

Pension and advanced underwriting specialist 169.167-058

Personnel analyst 166.267-018

Personnel scheduler 215.367-014

Portfolio strategist

Price economist 050.067-010

Process description writer 131.267-026

Productivity expert

Property accountant 160.167-022

Purchase price analyst 162.167-030

Real estate analyst or researcher

Real estate lawyer 110.117-034

Records management analyst 161.267-022

Reports analyst 161.267-026

Safety inspector 168.264-014

Social problems specialist 054.067-014

Software designer

Special risks insurance underwriter 169.167-058

Standard practice analyst 131.267-026

Systems accountant 160.167-026

Tax accountant 160.162-010

Tax attorney 110.117-038

Technical analyst

Title attorney 110.117-042

Title examiner 119.287-010

Title searcher 209.367-046

Translator 137.267-018

Wage and salary analyst

Professional and Trade Groups

American Accounting Association
American Association for Budget and
Program Analysis
American Bar Association
American Compensation Association
American Federation of Information
Processing Societies
American Institute of Certified Public
Accountants
American Society for Information Science
American Society of Pension Actuaries
American Statistical Association
Association for Systems Management

Association of the Institute for Certification
of Computer Professionals
Casualty Actuarial Society
Classification and Compensation Society
Financial Analysts Federation
Institute of Chartered Financial Analysts
National Association of Business Economists
National Association of Credit Management
National Association of Tax Practitioners
Operations Research Society of America
Society for Industrial and Applied
Mathematics
Society of Actuaries

Professional Reading

The American Economic Review
American Journal of Agricultural Economics
The American Statistician
The Appraisal Journal
Compensation and Benefits Review
The CPA Journal
Data Communications
Distribution
Dr. Dobb's Journal of Software Tools

The Economist
Employee Benefit Plan Review
The Engineering Economist
Financial Analysts Journal
Industrial Development and Site Selection
Handbook
Journal of Accountancy
Pension World
Risk Management
Trusts & Estates

Strong Aptitudes

GENERALIST *A frame of reference common to most people that facilitates coordination and compromise with others and emphasizes interpersonal skills*

Weak Reinforcing Aptitudes

IDEAPHORIA *An imaginative or creative ability useful in generating a rapid flow of ideas and brain-storming*

ANALYTICAL *A methodical type of problem-solving ability useful in organizing, coordinating, and planning*

DIAGNOSTIC *An intuitive type of problem-solving ability helpful in investigation and research*

PERCEPTUAL SPEED *The ability to perform computational and clerical work quickly and accurately*

STRUCTURAL VISUALIZATION *The ability to visualize structures in three dimensions*

Eight

The Delegators

Earl is a simply awful manager. His need to get involved in all the interesting projects—leaving only the routine "gopher" work for his subordinates—had already lead to confrontations with *his* boss, Mr. Frost.

Earl's most recent troubles were caused by his fascination with a rather long and complicated project that he had assigned to Chris, one of his better drafters. Chris, of course, only got the task because Earl was already involved in another project.

Chris stopped by Earl's desk early one Monday morning to give a progress report. A few minutes after the conversation, Earl called Chris back to his desk. His favorite pen was missing. Chris must have taken it. Earl told Chris to drop everything and find the pen. "I'm going to take a closer look at that project you've been working on," said Earl. "Keep hunting for that pen until you find it."

After looking under papers, on the floor, in and under drawers for a few minutes, Chris stormed into Mr. Frost's office with the story. In the company cafeteria, Mr. Frost asked Earl about Chris. Did the company have a kleptomaniac?

Earl chuckled. "Chris never will find that pen. I hid it. I guess I'll find it when I'm through doing my thing with Chris's project. It's really an interesting job, but it's a tough one. Chris is good, but this project looked like too much fun for me to pass up. I know I'll do a first-rate job, but I can't be sure that Chris would do it the way I would."

Mr. Frost had finally heard enough: "Earl, it's time for a change. Managing is just not your forte!"

An Abundance Of Riches

Earl is an excellent example of everything a natural Delegator is *not*—he simply has too *many* aptitudes to be an effective manager. Star player, yes. Coach, never. It was virtually impossible for him *not* to take over when a subordinate faltered...if he ever allowed the subordinate the chance to fail in the first place. His natural tendency for doing the work himself instead of managing others to get it done damaged his department's effectiveness.

As a Specialist, Earl had too narrow a perspective to relate well to his subordinates. He found it all-too-easy to devote himself single-mindedly to an engineering problem. Coaching his team of draftsmen to effectively and efficiently solve engineering and graphics snafus themselves was completely out of his league.

It was Earl's misfortune to typify the individual with *too many* aptitudes trying to be a Delegator, a profile characterized most by its *lack* of such strong aptitudes.

The paucity of strong aptitudes in the Delegator profile seems strange to a lot of people. But strong aptitudes demand *usage*. Think about what a good manager actually does—and about the difference between doing and delegating.

The remarkable fact about typical Delegators is that it is *not* an abundance of *strong* aptitudes that make them proficient managers; it's their glaring *deficiencies*. Most people get pleasure from using their aptitudes, and their jobs are more satisfying when they *can* use them. One of the most frustrating experiences for the misplaced manager is being able to do something well while overseeing a subordinate with less capability.

As a manager, if you decide it's easier to do the job yourself and take it out of the hands of your less-talented subordinates, you are not really managing.

If you let the subordinate perform the task you could have done better and faster, you are managing, but you're underutilizing your own aptitudes and getting an inferior job to boot.

Patience Is A Virtue

For many Delegators, their lack of strong aptitudes— while eventually making them excellent managers—will actually *inhibit* their rise to management. Most Delegators discover that the "fast track" up the corporate ladder is reserved for those who readily master their responsibilities, not for them. This reality can easily lead to frustration.

Elise is a typical Delegator. As a bank manager trainee, she took a lot longer to make it into management than many of her peers. But *un*like many Delegators, who become quickly frustrated at their comparatively slow progress, Elise did not become impatient—instead she continued to work to develop her abilities as an effective manager. Today, she is one of the bank's most reliable executives.

Elise's first year on the job was by far the most demanding. There was so much to learn!

Elise worked longer hours than she or her boss had anticipated. The routine reports and other paperwork took Elise longer than her boss thought it should—quite a bit longer, in fact, than it took other trainees. But her accuracy was amazingly good.

Despite Elise's relatively slow pace, her boss was pleased with her performance. Her way of thinking was good for the organization. She wasn't a perfectionist, but she didn't let real problems become chronic ones. What he was observing were the effects of her Generalist outlook and her low aptitudes.

Elise's Diagnostic aptitude, for example, was weak, which meant she was not immediately critical of others and exhibited a much more patient and accepting attitude than most people. This trait enhanced her relationship with other staffers and with her organization. Elise did not automatically pinpoint inefficiencies—she was more prone to carry out procedures than to question their efficacy, rarely finding fault with her fellow workers or with the bank's overall structure or operations.

It took Elise twelve years to reach the branch management position she now holds. Most of the bank's manager trainees moved up much faster, and Elise couldn't help but notice that she was falling behind in her climb up the corporate ladder.

But whenever she asked her superiors about her slow progress, they consistently encouraged her to stay. They were honest with her, and her years of persistent effort paid off. Her limited number of aptitudes may have slowed her rise in the company, but they did not *prevent* it.

The factor that kept Elise persevering in spite of her limited aptitudes was her strong self-esteem, a factor not uncommon to many Delegators. Over the course of her career, Elise developed the confidence that she could master *any* task if she worked long and hard enough—a vital strategy for success as a Delegator. Unless a Delegator is willing to "pay the price" of working longer and harder than his or her peers, he or she is destined to struggle in low level jobs.

Like Elise, those Delegators that invest their time and energies in learning a profession can become very productive managers. The weak aptitudes that will probably slow their progress lower down the ladder can become vital assets when they finally make it into management.

But remember: *Being* a manager and *getting* into management usually require different aptitudes. Delegators *must* devote much more time and effort to jobs on the way *to* management than their colleagues...and have the patience to persist until they reach their goals.

Push Those Papers

Remember the long hours Elise spent completing the paperwork part of her job? Her boss noticed that reports took more of her time than expected. Again, her aptitudes were reflected in her job performance. Elise is not strong in Perceptual Speed, which means she cannot quickly complete tasks involving computational and clerical work without making a lot of mistakes. So she proceeded slowly.

A cursory glance at most beginning positions in business reveals that many *do* require extensive clerical work. Conventional wisdom has it that paper pushing and number crunching teach the neophyte the basics about a business. Most Delegators with minimal aptitudes "cut their teeth" in these pedestrian roles, ones in which their lack of Perceptual Speed make paperwork an arduous task, indeed.

Sales: An Escape From Paperwork

An *extroverted* Delegator may find sales an attractive alternate route. Selling puts the novice in a position to learn a business by getting familiar with its clients' needs and its competitors. For many sales positions, the extroverted Delegator's vibrant personality is the only prerequisite.

Diane exemplifies the Extrovert Delegator who chose sales as a route into management. Today she is a successful sales manager with an office equipment firm. It took her a while, unfortunately, to discover this alternate route: Sales was not her first choice, but an avenue that opened up only after she spent five years "pushing paper" as a secretary. Her boss's last performance review made it obvious a change was long overdue:

> Diane, you spend too much time talking and too much time away from your desk. When customers phone, you take ten or fifteen minutes to find out what they need. I don't

know what you talk about—you've never even met these people!

You spend so much time socializing with the other secretaries that they don't get their work done. When I need to ask you something or need you to type a letter, half the time I can't even find you. Where would we be if the secretaries couldn't find the office manager when they needed her? Another thing is that you can never work overtime when we get into a bind. You always have a club meeting, a party, or some other outside activity.

Diane, all of this might surprise you, and I know it sounds very harsh. The reason I haven't brought it up before is that you are such a likable person. We all enjoy being around you. But you're not a secretary, and you're not an office manager. If you really want to get ahead in life, you ought to think about sales. You're just like those guys.

Diane cornered a couple of salespeople and asked them about their work. It didn't sound bad. They spent a lot of time talking to people and were out and about most of the time. The fact that the bulk of their paychecks depended on commissions bothered Diane, but it was obvious that they made a lot more money than she did.

The more she talked to them, the more she realized that her boss was right: She had a lot more in common with the salespeople than with her secretarial co-workers.

Diane asked her boss for a recommendation to the sales manager. She happily consented—she liked Diane, but was now anxious to get her out of the department. An extroverted secretary who realized she had a dead-end job meant trouble.

Diane spent a lot of time preparing for her interview with the sales manager. She borrowed a blue suit from a friend and tried to look as professional as possible. She practiced shaking hands with her friend and "role played" answers to a number of questions she expected would crop up in the interview.

The sales manager's first impression of Diane was a good one. "At least she looks all right for the job," he thought. He asked her why she wanted to change to sales and why she thought she'd be successful. Diane recounted her talks with the two salespeople. She told the sales manager that everything they had told her made her confident that she was right for the job. "And five years as a secretary here have given me a lot of product knowledge," Diane added. "Teach me how to sell and I'll work harder than anybody."

After talking with the two salespeople Diane mentioned, both of whom had been impressed with Diane's drive, the sales manager agreed to give her a chance.

It took Diane five years to discover she wasn't a secretary. It took her only *three* years to earn the company's prize for top sales producer. Unlike many of her sales colleagues, Diane had not brought in a great number of new accounts. Nor had she particularly tried to do so.

But she had made more frequent calls on her regular customers and used her secretarial experience to recommend a wider variety of the products her company sold, all of which she could demon-strate. She sold more products to more accounts more often—a winning formula in any sales situation!

When Diane learned she was being considered for sales management, she signed up for evening courses in management theory, supervisory techniques, and organizational psychology at a local college and joined a professional organization, all of which increased her confidence that she could handle increased managerial responsibilities.

Given her sales record and the moves she made to prepare for management, no one could think of a good reason why she *shouldn't* move into management.

Diane's Delegator personality is perfect for her new role. At least once a week she accompanies each of her salespeople on their calls. She finds that her salespeople are more productive if she talks to them frequently and keeps their morale up. Diane is able to motivate them in these face-to-face communications.

She has a secretary who processes a large portion of the reports and other paperwork that are part of her new job. Diane is managing effectively, even though she is away from her desk and talking to people most of the time.

This mode of operation works because she is managing salespeople, not secretaries.

Introverts & Extroverts

If you are a Delegator, it's important you understand the difference between Diane, the sales manager, and Elise, the bank branch manager.

If you are an Introvert or Ambivert like Elise, you should avoid sales positions. The jobs for which you would qualify likely will require many cold calls and demand high volume sales. Your lack of interpersonal skills will subvert your productivity and progress in most companies.

But if you are an Extrovert like Diane, sales is the right choice.

Particular Problems You Must Face

Introverts and Ambiverts do not go out of their way to "toot their own horns." When they accomplish a laudable goal in the organization, they refrain from drawing attention to their success. Peers and bosses alike remain oblivious, applauding instead those employees who make sure everyone knows when *they* achieve something.

Introverts must find a comfortable way of making sure the right people know about their achievements and overcome their feelings that such self promotion is pretentious.

Such an opportunity may occur, for example, during a performance review, in which one can tactfully express the satisfaction of reaching a particular goal or completing a difficult project.

Another approach to this insecurity is to cultivate one-to-one relationships with influential people. Singling out a superior and providing loyal service to him or her can open doors that the Introvert has trouble opening himself. Such a "mentor" or "rabbi" can act as a buffer and smooth the Introvert's career path.

If you are painfully shy or unusually submissive, something must be done to correct the problem early on. The management position to which you may aspire—and, as a

Delegator, be perfectly suited for—will be an unobtainable goal if nothing is done.

Avoiding the attention of others or giving undue deference to people is self-defeating for any would-be manager. Taking an assertiveness training course may help; sometimes individual counseling or psychotherapy may be necessary.

Learning to speak to large groups and to give presentations to colleagues and bosses are necessary experiences for the introverted manager trainee.

The Introvert (and sometimes the Ambivert) must take special care to be approachable. Some co-workers will interpret their introspective, reserved natures as a signal to stay away.

The easiest way to remedy this situation is to go out of your way to assure your subordinates and colleagues of your accessibility. *Telling* an assistant or a secretary to come in and talk if there is a problem that needs to be discussed (as opposed to *assuming* they'll know that) is a simple solution. Arranging definite times to meet with colleagues on an ongoing basis will underscore your availability.

One Introvert solved this "approachability" problem with a red cap, simply telling everyone that the only time they should *not* come into his office or stop him in the corridor to talk was when he wore his red cap. The cap was his nonverbal signal that he had to devote his full attention to a project or report and shouldn't be unnecessarily disturbed.

Dress For Success

Delegators, especially introverted ones, benefit more than most other business types from learning how to dress properly and how to handle business entertainment. The business world is one of impressions, so a sharp appearance and proper manners are important for anyone.

But they are especially important for Delegators.

If your bosses have second thoughts about how fast you are picking up on things—and your lack of aptitudes ensures you will be slower than many of your peers—they certainly do not need their doubts reinforced by your sloppy dress and bad etiquette.

Find A Springboard

The reason that some Delegators fail is that they cannot find a company with the right sort of training program. *And Delegators need training programs.* The right dress, good interview preparation, and an impressive resume do little good if a Delegator winds up in a company lacking such a program.

Larger companies have more structured management training programs that often include classroom instruction and seminars combined with on-the-job training. Some have coordinated their training programs with evening graduate schools of business at local universities. Companies with such well-planned training for their managers are a boon to Delegators.

Delegators can use the military as a springboard, too. The military offers courses in personnel relations, accounting, contract law, operations research, and many other fields.

A college degree is usually necessary to qualify for those military positions that prepare you for management in private industry. Many ex-military people who depended on their high school diplomas and technical training from the military for good jobs in civilian life have been disappointed. A college degree will help you be taken seriously, whether or not you join one of the military services.

Welcome To The Frying Pan

Beware of the small company that requires its managers to take on a wide variety of duties. In such situations, you must wear a number of different hats, one of which belongs to the fireman.

Since procedures at small enterprises are less rigid than at larger firms, some things arc ncglected until they become crises. These crises are the "fires" that you, as a manager, must control. Lurching from one crisis to the next is not the way a Delegator develops competence.

As a "jack of all trades," you may never master any. And, as we've seen, it's especially important for the Delegator to develop expertise in specific areas.

Checklist For Success

If you're a Delegator, you would be well advised to consider the following list *specific criteria* for selecting a career. Considering these factors prerequisites for accepting an offer will help prevent the failure they have brought upon many other Delegators:

Make certain you do not have more aptitudes than you need for the position you want. *You do not need many aptitudes to be a Delegator.* An unused aptitude *lessens* your job satisfaction.

Be ready to work *harder* and *longer* than most other people during the learning phases of the job.

Think about whether you are an Extrovert, Introvert or Ambivert. Look for an entry-level position that *matches your personality.*

Develop *good grooming, dress, and business etiquette.* Take courses, read books, and/or see a consultant if you are deficient in this area.

Look for companies with *structured training programs*; these will generally be larger firms. Which is why you should...

Be wary of small companies.

Delegator Business Careers

Administrative services manager
169.167-034

Aquatic facility manager 187.167-054

Association executive 189.117-010

Bank branch manager 186.117-038

Branch manager 183.117-010

Casino manager 187.167-070

Club manager 187.167-126

College financial aid administrator
090.117-030

College or university business manager
186.117-010

College registrar 090.167-030

Commissary manager 185.167-010

Contingents supervisor 205.367-050

Correspondence section supervisor
(insurance) 249.137-018

Credit and collection manager 168.167-054

Credit authorizer 249.367-022

Credit union manager 186.167-026

Data control clerk supervisor 219.137-014

Day care center manager

Delivery department supervisor
230.137-014

Dental, laboratory manager 187.167-090

Department manager 189.167-022

Department store manager 185.117-010

Dude ranch manager 187.167-094

Employment agency manager 187.167-098

Employment manager 166.167-030

Files supervisor 206.137-010

Film vault supervisor 222.137-010

Finance company manager 186.117-038

Financial institution manager 186.117-038

Financial institution president 186.117-054

Fish and game club manager 187.167-102

Fish hatchery supervisor 446.134-010

Floor manager 299.137-010

Food concession manager 185.167-022

Forest nursery supervisor 451.137-010

Front office manager (hotel and restaurant)
187.167-110

Game farm supervisor 412.131-010

Gate services supervisor (air
transportation) 238.137-018

General manager 183.117-014

Golf club manager 187.167-114

Health club manager 339.137-010

Hospital admitting officer 205.137-010

Hotel recreational facilities manager
187.167-122

Insurance office manager 186.167-034

Loan closer (financial institution)
249.367-050

Machinery or equipment rental and leasing
manager 185.167-026

Management trainee 189.167-018

Military officer

Mortgage banking company manager
186.117-038

Nursing home superintendent

Office manager 169.167-034

Order department supervisor 169.167-038

Park superintendent

Personnel administrator

Postmaster 189.167-066

President 189.117-026

Program manager 189.167-030

Public events facilities rental manager
186.117-062

Rate supervisor 214.137-018

Recreation establishment manager
187.117-042
Reservations manager 238.137-010
Retail store manager 185.167-046
Savings and loan association manager
186.117-038
Schools superintendent 099.117-022
Security officer 189.167-034
Service superintendent (hotel and
restaurant) 329.137-010

Social service or welfare administrator
Stock supervisor 221.137-034
Theater manager 187.167-158
Treasurer 161.117-018
Trust accounts supervisor (financial
institution) 219.132-014
Trust company manager 186.117-038
Underwriting clerks supervisor (insurance)
219.132-022

Professional and Trade Groups

Administrative Management Society
American Assoc. of School Administrators
American Bankers Association
American Business Women's Association
American College of Healthcare Executives
American Hotel and Motel Association
American Management Association
American Soc. for Personnel Administration
American Society for Public Administration
American Society of Association Executives

Club Managers Association of America
Employment Management Association
National Association for Female Executives
National Association of Church Business
Administration
National Association of Credit Management
National Management Association
National Recreation and Park Association
National Retail Merchants Association

Professional Reading

ABA Banker's Weekly
Administrative Management
Apparel Industry Magazine
Association Management
Bank Administration
Chain Store Executive
Contract Management
Credit Union Magazine
Discount Merchandiser
Electronic Business

Executive Female
Furniture World
Health Care Management
Hospitals
Human Resource Management
International Management
Personnel Administrator
Personnel Management
Stores
Working Woman

EXTROVERT *An outgoing, sociable, somewhat impulsive personality*

IDEAPHORIA *An imaginative or creative ability useful in generating a rapid flow of ideas and brain-storming*

ANALYTICAL *A methodical type of problem-solving ability useful in organizing, coordinating, and planning*

DIAGNOSTIC *An intuitive type of problem-solving ability helpful in investigation and research*

Weak Reinforcing
Aptitudes

FORESIGHT *The ability to see long-term possibilities and be motivated by rewards that may lie far in the future.*

Nine

The Wheeler-Dealers

It's dreary near the Miami waterfront. On the light-less street corner, two men exchange brown paper bags, one presumably filled with drugs , the other with cash. As the buy goes down, Crockett and Tubbs screech into the scene in their Ferrari, busting buyer and seller as they consummate their deal. Wheeler-Dealers on TV.

That same evening, Michael Milken is the subject of every TV station's lead story on the evening newscast—he is being indicted for insider trading in what is fast becoming an ongoing saga of Wall Street greed and corruption. The Junk Bond King, who nearly single-handedly initiated the crazed market for takeovers and leveraged buyouts. Wheeler-Dealers in the news.

No, Wheeler-Dealers have not been kindly treated by the media lately. Whether it's the corner drug deal, insider trading scandals, or the latest influence-peddling scandal on Capitol Hill, the media has made us increasingly aware of Wheeler-Dealers who are unscrupulously exploiting us for their own avaricious ends.

Despite this media blitz, it must be clearly understood that there are many *legitimate* Wheeler-Dealers, those unique individuals with a particular talent for bringing buyer and seller together and "making the deal." Indeed, the legion of legitimate Wheeler-Dealers perform a vital function in today's business world—bringing together those with a need and those who can satisfy it.

Unfortunately, the media has slighted these legitimate Wheeler-Dealers. Few television shows, movies or books accurately detail the myriad deals made by investment bankers, floor brokers, business brokers, or the many other Wheeler-Dealers functioning well within the realm of the law. These scrupulous professionals are routinely overshadowed by the handful involved in the scandals and rip-offs highlighted by the media.

Though highly illegal and a bit unconventional, the Wheeler-Dealer familiar to most people is the drug dealer. I will use it as an example for people who have had little real-life or vicarious experience with other Wheeler-Dealers, but this "occupation" is obviously *not* one I endorse or recommend.

There is a lot more involved in making a drug deal than exchanging "product" for cash. The dealer must use his intuition to size up suppliers and buyers, get a "feel" for how to handle each of them, then use all his negotiating skills to work out terms acceptable to both sides. When the trade takes place, careful sampling of the drug shows that the dealer knows his product. Arrangement for more trades come if the dealer establishes a reliable reputation.

The negotiating skill, detailed knowledge of the product, and strong reputation of the dealer are the very same characteristics essential to Wheeler-Dealers involved with legitimate products.

A friend of mine once knew a drug dealer who told him, "In this business, you get out, you get bigger, or you get busted." Needless to say, there are significant drawbacks to this kind of life. Luckily, the threat to life and limb from dissatisfied buyers and sellers, the chance of spending some time in prison, and the moral questions involved do not play a role in the lives of most Wheeler-Dealers.

Team Players Need Not Apply

Legitimate Wheeler-Dealers share many characteristics with the Persuaders and Communicators described in Chapters 3 and 5. In fact, many Wheeler-Dealers started their careers in the sales occupations that fit the Persuaders; a few started in Communicator occupations.

Unlike these other two personality types, the Wheeler-Dealer generally looks to operate in an independent fashion. Wheeler-Dealers typically work in less structured situations than Persuaders and Communicators. Their strong Analytical and/or Diagnostic aptitudes help them deal with the fluid nature of this kind of work environment. Wheeler-Dealers tend to structure situations as they experience them. Some of them feel pure pleasure when they can let a situation take on a life of its own, make up their own rules, and wind up with an unconventional but terrific deal.

Often described as "loners," Wheeler-Dealers—Specialists or not—simply find that most corporate structures and organizational rules confine them. Unusual creativity or upbringing or unconventional attitudes preclude their fitting into typical corporate teams. A lot of Wheeler-Dealers become loners because they want elbow room to wheel and deal with freedom.

Adam is such a loner—an extroverted Specialist. He's one of those people in constant motion, even when he's sitting in a chair. In addition to the normal complement of Wheeler-Dealer aptitudes, he has strong Perceptual Speed and strong Number Memory.

As a commodities-futures trader at the New York Mercantile Exchange, he "deals" for himself—using his own money to buy and sell contracts. Adam never actually takes delivery of the commodities he trades, but takes advantage of price fluctuations to make profits. Here's how he describes himself:

> I guess I'm a lone wolf in the midst of all this hubbub. There are so many things I like about this life! I'm my own boss. That's important. I don't have to depend on other people to get ahead. That's what drove me crazy when I was accounts receivable manager for a big manufacturing firm.
>
> I came up with some great ideas for a credit screening system, then I had to depend on the statisticians and computer programmers to get the thing into motion. Those people can be real prima donnas, and I just didn't have the patience for them.
>
> That company had a big problem with past due accounts, so I stepped up collection efforts. All I got were complaints from the sales department that I was upsetting their customers. You try to do your job, and all these other people set up roadblocks for you. That's not for me.
>
> Now I can depend on myself and reap the rewards of my efforts. And this place jumps. It's fun to yell, scream, jump up and down. Things move fast. It looks like chaos to some people; but for me, it's great.
>
> It's a lot better than trudging into the office, pasting a smile on your face, being nice to your boss, remembering your secretary's birthday, and trying to keep everybody happy—at least the ones who can take you down a notch if you don't lick their boots. I look at my old company's headquarters now and see that it was a tomb for me—quiet and lifeless.

Adam's self-description reveals key factors about his aptitudes—a profile not atypical of many Wheeler-Dealers. Like many other Extroverts, Adam has a rather aggressive personality. His action-oriented nature augments his performance in the dynamic environment of the pits, a place where hesitation and a soft voice lose the day.

Responding positively to "all this hubbub," as he describes his work environment, typifies Extroverts. Adam's distaste for depending on other people in an organizational setting is shared by many other Specialists. (This need for independence is not unique to Specialists. Some Generalists prefer to work independently too, but they do not find it as critical to career success as Specialists.)

How Big A Risk Are *You* Ready For?

Adam has no great fear of taking risks, a trait that has little to do with his aptitudes, but a necessity for him and most other Wheeler-Dealers, many of whom work on a commission-only basis or make money only if they make enough profitable trades. (There are also elements of risk in the careers of the Entrepreneurs, Consultants, and Small Business Owners discussed in Chapters 10, 11, and 12.)

Your propensity for risk-taking depends more on demographics and psychographics—how you were raised, your family circumstances, your personal experiences—than on your aptitudes. If you are either an immigrant or the oldest child in your family, you are in a group statistically more likely to take business risks. Whether your parents succeeded or failed when *they* took risks will also influence your feelings about risk-raking. If your family and friends prize government and big company jobs for their security, their attitudes might very well discourage your own plunge into a job or career laden with more visible risk.

For the Wheeler-Dealer, there are two important considerations when thinking about the concept of risk.

One is that *most successful risk-takers have some probability of success when they embark on a venture. They do not take the risk when the odds tell them they will almost surely lose.*

Risk-takers who always play long shots—ventures promising minimal chances for a pay-off—may well have a pathological need to be losers. They might fear success, think they don't deserve it, or like to punish themselves.

There are also people who take ill-fated risks because they have deluded themselves with their own grandiosity— they have convinced themselves they have an immunity to the odds.

Successful risk-takers not only take risks that have reasonable chances of success, *they also have specific knowledge or skills that help to diminish the odds against them.* Because of what the risk-taker knows and others do not, a situation that seems to be terribly chancy really might not be too risky at all.

Outsiders might look at the situation and shudder at the peril they see. The successful risk-taker will know enough about the details, context, and possible outcomes to feel comfortable with the level of risk involved.

Abigail is such a Wheeler-Dealer, one who has awed friends and family with what *they* call outlandish speculation. An athletic-looking woman with a purposeful walk and a self-confident bearing, Abigail is a commercial real estate broker who has prospered tremendously from such "speculative" deals, earning hefty commissions on the sakes she arranges.

What makes her loved ones uncomfortable is the amount of her own money Abigail puts into these real estate ventures. A couple of years ago, for example, she used more than half her previous year's income for down payments on a dozen rather shabby, forty-year old frame houses.

First of all, no one in Abigail's circle of acquaintances would live in such a place. But to top it off, a strip shopping center with a *topless bar* formed one of the boundaries of the neighborhood!

When Abigail rented the houses to an assortment of refugees from Southeast Asia, college students, and recently-divorced young mothers, even her friends started referring to her as "The Slum Lady." They did not realize the extent of Abigail's real estate knowledge. She explains her reasons for taking this "risk":

> It all started because I was actually in the process of finding a buyer for that sleazy shopping center. I drove around the area to get a feel for the neighborhood. These frame houses were the first things that hit my eyes. Boy! Was that depressing! How could I convince a client of the shopping center's potential when the closest possible shoppers lived in houses with peeling paint, crumbled-up sidewalks, and weeds and broken beer bottles in their yards?

Fortunately, I kept driving. On the streets immediately north and west, I found old places built in the twenties and thirties. Many were being renovated. I had no doubt that scores of illegal aliens from south of the border shared some of the apartments that a few of these places had been divided into. But what impressed me was the number of places that had been fixed up—BMWs and Audis graced *these* driveways. A bundle had gone into landscaping. Gentrification at work!

Heading back to the office, I avoided the rush-hour traffic on the freeways and discovered that you could get downtown in less than fifteen minutes on a secondary thoroughfare. I felt a lot better about selling the strip shopping center to someone besides my worst enemy, because I was convinced that Yuppies would surround it before long.

I found the right buyers—a 40-year-old lawyer and her architect-husband—and I think they actually speeded up the changes in the neighborhood.

The woman has always been an active feminist. She plans to boot out the topless bar as soon as their lease expires.

Her husband grew up in Philadelphia, where neighborhood restaurants are part of the scenery. He has designed and will oversee a remodeling project to give the whole place some character. That should attract small restaurant owners. They're already talking to an Italian restaurateur and a natural foods eatery about locating there. Considering the neighborhood, an Oriental restaurant will probably pop up, too.

An outfit called "Not Quite Antiques" will move in next week. They sell good quality used furniture on consignment. When I saw what the lawyer-architect couple was doing with the shopping center, I realized the potential in these disheveled frame houses and bought them.

It wasn't their value as houses that appealed to me. It was their proximity to the neighborhood to the northwest and to the downtown area that made them a good investment. The changes in the shopping center would make the location more acceptable, too. Now I'm talking to a developer about buying my houses, razing the "slum," and building pricey townhouses.

Abigail is still taking a calculated risk, but her knowledge of real estate in general and this area in particular have significantly reduced the downside potential.

Her skill in finding buyers to whom the shopping center would appeal augmented her chances of success. Abigail is behaving as any successful risk-taker would and using her Wheeler-Dealer aptitudes.

Patience Is Not Affordable

One thing to notice about both Abigail and Adam is that their success does not depend on many years of following through on their ideas. Their rewards are rather immediate, and neither involves themselves in long-term projects: Abigail receives commissions on the deals she puts together. Adam profits on his trades in a matter of minutes or hours.

Abigail is looking for someone else to buy her rent houses and give her a reasonably quick profit. She herself will not develop the up-and-coming area. While she can convince a developer of the potential of the area because *she* can see it, developing it herself would not only involve her in some management and coordination tasks she dislikes, but also delay the profit she will realize.

Abigail and Adam both have weak Foresight aptitude. Immediate rewards gratify them more than the possibilities of long-term rewards. Their preference for quick returns and their extroverted personalities predispose Wheeler-Dealers to initiate and consummate deals quickly. Their action-oriented aptitudes are ideal for pushing negotiations to a rapid conclusion.

The strong Ideaphoria and Analytical or Diagnostic aptitudes characteristic of Wheeler-Dealers also reflect their bias for action.

The Art Of The Deal

The predominant activity for typical Wheeler-Dealers is bringing a potential buyer to the table with a seller. Within this context, the Wheeler-Dealer operates as a negotiator and consultant working to satisfy the interests of both parties. The reputation they build for harmonizing the buyer's need and the seller's want opens doors to future deals. Success often depends on their renown as negotiators.

Although they do not work with people in an organizational setting, they use their communicating and creative problem-solving aptitudes in negotiating with clients. They are adroit in fashioning the terms of a deal, sometimes spontaneously.

Benjamin epitomizes the artful negotiator. In addition to the usual complement of Wheeler-Dealer aptitudes, he has Structural Visualization, the aptitude for spatial or three-dimensional thinking, and Associative Memory, an aptitude helpful in learning foreign languages.

He brokers various kinds of industrial machinery. His sellers are companies that have bought updated equipment and want to sell their old equipment, his buyers foreign companies in lesser-developed countries.

Recently he approached a Mexican company that had expressed interest in used printing equipment. As usual, he mentioned an approximate price less than that of state-of-the-art equipment but more than what he anticipated the final selling price to be.

The Mexican businessmen pointed out that no one in their company knew how to operate a different type of printing equipment. Additionally, payment would be slow since operations would be shut down while the newly-acquired equipment was being installed and workers trained.

Benjamin confidently assured them that he could come up with a deal they liked. At that point, he had no idea of what he could do for them, but he knew he could create some kind of salable deal. Here's how he did it:

> I called up the guys I know who sell the new high tech printing equipment with all the bells and whistles. I told them I had a buyer for their customers' old stuff. This was good news for them, since they're more likely to make a sale of new equipment if someone is ready to buy the *old* equipment and help defray the expense.
> I also talked to the guys who handle bad loans at some of the larger banks to see if they had any printers going belly up. I mentioned a price lower than I thought they'd actually get and told them that finding and paying for a Spanish-speaking trainer was the only possible hitch in the deal.

I didn't say anything about the terms of payment, because I've learned that once you get them to agree on a price, coming up with a payment schedule is easy.

One of the new equipment salesmen got back to me and said he had a possible seller, a huge printing plant out near Los Angeles. He told me the price I wanted to pay was a little low and he didn't know any Spanish-speaking people who operated the equipment.

This was pretty much what I expected, so I proposed that his client pay for a trip for a bilingual person from my Mexican client company. My buyer could send one of his people to the seller's plant while the old equipment was still in operation, and he could learn how to set it up and operate it.

Since I speak Spanish fluently, I could be on hand for at least one day to straighten out any communications problems. The seller could raise the price of the equipment to cover the cost of the trip, and the buyer could benefit from the training and enjoy a "free" trip to Los Angeles, home of Disneyland and numerous other attractions. Everybody was happy so far.

The Los Angeles company agreed to wait four months for payment, and the Mexican company agreed to a much higher price than I expected...after we made arrangements for *three* of their people to visit Los Angeles. I took a percent less commission than I usually take because the luxury travel expenses for the Mexican buyers were built into the selling price, and the Los Angeles company spent a lot of time training the new owners.

I felt good about this deal. The Mexicans got equipment they could afford. The Los Angeles company realized some dollars from their old equipment. I speeded up a sale for the new equipment salesman.

I did a lot of jawboning to get everyone to agree on things, but it was worth it. This deal would have never happened without *me.*

Benjamin's explanation zeroes in on the psychological reward he gets from negotiating a deal. When he performs his job successfully, nothing is created. It has simply changed hands. But both the buyer and the seller benefit from the trade.

The economic value of the Wheeler-Dealers to the rest of the world lies in their ability to find buyers and sellers who might not otherwise find each other. The buyer should be able to use the goods to be traded more productively than the seller, and the seller should realize more from the proceeds of the sale than from the use of the goods themselves. The Wheeler-Dealer should get pleasure and money for making the deal happen.

Knowing When To Run

The joy a Wheeler-Dealer gets from making a deal has been known to cause problems. Sometimes he becomes so enamored with the idea of doing the "deal of the century" that he fails to adequately analyze its relative merits. The psychology of winning—or "closing a deal"—may take precedence over the real benefits of the deal for buyer and seller. This tendency is one of the reasons Wheeler-Dealers fail.

It is graphically illustrated by the case of Art, who made his living buying mineral rights from landowners in strategic locations, putting together a convincing presentation about their possibilities for oil and gas production, and selling them to major companies for a profit and an override on future production.

A business acquaintance introduced Art to a broker who was trying to find a buyer for a pipeline system in the Northeast. This broker suggested that Art might want to diversify into the transporting of natural gas as protection against a downturn in his current business. Art launched into his Wheeler-Dealer behavior to see how good a deal he could make.

The other broker enjoyed deal-making as much as Art, so over the next few weeks, they haggled over price, terms of payment, guarantees on contracts from gas producers, and improvements to the metering system. Though Art realized the asking price was already low, he was excited at the prospect of negotiating an even lower price and getting a number of concessions from the seller.

The two brokers played a chess-like game of wits. The pipeline system became an excuse to see who could "win" a particular term of the deal. Art became so intent on making the greatest deal of the century that he failed to realize the folly of his actually *owning* that pipeline system.

Because owning it was not a particularly great idea. It would require additional office staff and space. Art would have to function as administrator and manager and make decisions involving some technical knowledge of gas-gathering systems he did not have. These changes would impinge on Art's effectiveness as an independent landman. Not until his banker pointed out that the present owners spent most of their time operating the system did Art realize that the deal was a bad one for him.

With his banker's cold-hearted analysis and its accompanying jolt of reality, Art came to his senses and halted negotiations. Now he cringes every time he recalls his near-miss. He almost became a victim of his own deal-making ability.

If you're a Wheeler-Dealer, remember Art's experience. Making the deal is *not* an end in itself. If your client suffers from a pointless deal, you tarnish your reputation. If, like Art, you are about to become a buyer in one of your own deals, step back and try to be completely rational about its advantages and disadvantages.

Con Artists Beware

Another cause for failure among Wheeler-Dealers is the same as that discussed for Persuaders—they acquire only a superficial knowledge of the products or services they trade but try to con prospective clients into seeing them as experts. If this lack of knowledge doesn't affect them immediately, it will eventually.

One pitfall for these Wheeler-Dealers occurs when their would-be clients figure out that they really do *not* know what they are talking about. A client who senses that the Wheeler-Dealer is running a con will likely retreat from the deal. But as they withdraw, they may feel so betrayed that they report the Wheeler-Dealer to the local governing agencies.

A second pitfall for the Wheeler-Dealer relying on only superficial understanding happens when a completed deal goes sour. When clients find hidden faults with the product or service after the fact, they often initiate lawsuits or even criminal prosecution. The Wheeler-Dealer who tries to succeed on basic talent and personality alone quickly receives the "used-car salesman" reputation—especially when he victimizes a client with his ignorance.

What's A Broker To Do?

Stockbrokers are a group that fails to fit neatly into the Wheeler-Dealer category—or any other category described in this book—though it seems it *should*. Until the late seventies, stockbrokers matched the Communicator description in Chapter 5—counseling their clients on financial matters, discussing the advantages and disadvantages of various investments, and executing buy and sell orders from their clients. Their commissions came from the trades they arranged, just as they do today. Analyzing their clients' portfolios and finding more attractive investment opportunities resulted in a continuing stream of commissions for stockbrokers.

Today brokerage firms, especially the large ones, put more pressure on their brokers to *sell*. Beginning stockbrokers with no established clients find they are expected to perform as Persuaders. They have quotas to meet. Analyzing clients' needs seems to fall to the bottom of their list of priorities almost immediately.

As the recipient of daily telephone solicitations from stockbrokers of major national firms, I am astonished at their ignorance. The dissonance I feel when such a stockbroker gives inane answers to very basic questions about the investment being touted is, I believe, a reflection of the dissonance inherent in the job.

It might be that most stockbrokers of the future will deal with institutional investors as clients. They might then function as Wheeler-Dealers. On the other hand, the institutional investors might simply employ their own negotiators to buy and sell their securities. Then again, the job of stockbroker might disappear altogether.

Wheeler-Dealer Checklist

If you are a Wheeler-Dealer, keep these guidelines in mind. They spell the difference between success and failure:

Acquire more than a superficial knowledge of your product or service. You will probably need to work under someone or as an employee before you gain enough competence to strike out on your own.

Think twice about becoming a stockbroker. Better yet, think ten times.

Making a deal for the sake of making a deal is a bad deal. Don't let the talent that makes you a success—being able to make a deal—turn you into a failure. Be certain that there is a realistic basis for the deal to be made.

If it has no benefits for your clients, it damages your reputation. Aim your ability to wheel and deal at situations that truly need you. One highly successful business broker put it this way: "I don't create companies; I bring together companies that need one another. When that happens, I've helped both become better off than they were before."

Wheeler-Dealer Business Careers

Arbitrageur
Auctioneer
Broker
Business broker
Business opportunity and property investment broker 187.167-018
Commodities futures trader
Factorer 186.117-026
Floor broker or floor trader 162.157-014
Independent business broker

Independent investment broker
Independent manufacturers' representative
Independent oil and gas landman
Investment banker
Literary agent
Real estate broker
Real estate sales person
Talent agent
Ticket broker

Professional and Trade Groups

American Association of Commodity Traders
American Stock Exchange
Association of Ship Brokers and Agents
Association of Talent Agents
Chicago Board of Trade
Chicago Mercantile Exchange
Hotel and Motel Brokers of America
Independent Literary Agents Association
International Association of Transport
   Aircraft Brokers
International Business Brokers Association
International Traders Association
Livestock Marketing Association
Manufacturers Agents National Association

Manufacturers Representatives of America
National Association of Realtors
National Auctioneers Association
National Auto Auction Association
National Food Brokers Association
New York Mercantile Exchange
New York Stock Exchange
Securities Industry Association
Society of Authors' Representatives
Society of Manufacturers Representatives
Transportation Brokers Conference of
   America
Yacht Architect and Brokers Association

Professional Reading

Auction and Surplus
Euromoney
Futures: The Magazine of Commodities and
   Options

Investment Dealer's Digest
Landman
Opportunity
Real Estate Today

Strong
Aptitudes

IDEAPHORIA *An imaginative or creative ability useful in generating a rapid flow of ideas and brain-storming*

ANALYTICAL *A methodical type of problem-solving ability useful in organizing, coordinating, and planning*

DIAGNOSTIC *An intuitive type of problem-solving ability helpful in investigation and research*

FORESIGHT *The ability to see long-term possibilities and be motivated by rewards that may lie far in the future.*

Weak Reinforcing
Aptitudes

NONE OR ANY, *depending on type of business*

Ten

The Entrepreneurs

Until recently felled by illness, Sam Walton, at age 67, was as active in his company as ever. He visited all his stores —and many of his *competitors'* stores—at least once a year. He even led cheers at store openings!

Despite the fact that his Wal-Mart stock was valued at over $2.5 billion, Walton was never a conspicuous consumer —he drove himself between stores in his own Ford pick-up.

A typical, though abnormally successful, Entrepreneur, Walton spent twenty years single-mindedly devoting himself to building an empire of budget stores. His only outside interests were his family, tennis, and bird hunting, but his intensity and perseverance obviously paid off quite handsomely.

Beyond The Glitz

Entrepreneur! The word conjures up images of wild ideas, daredevil risks, heroic action, and billion-dollar pay-offs. Names like Steve Jobs, Ross Perot, and Ted Turner awe us. Best-selling books laud their feats and sing their praises. Inspired, many rush off to the patent offices with the next widget that will change the world.

If this is your perception of the Entrepreneur, reality may be very harsh. As you read this chapter and brush away the glitz, you will realize that Entrepreneurs like these didn't just get crazy and lucky at the same time. Each had an idea, organized a business around it, figured out how to make money from it, and stuck with it over a period of many years. Each took a risk, worked long and hard—may even have failed several times—before turning a profit.

Like the Wheeler-Dealers of Chapter 9, Entrepreneurs are aggressive types with creative problem-solving abilities who are not averse to taking risks. And like Wheeler-Dealers, Entrepreneurs function poorly in static organizations.

What separates Entrepreneurs from Wheeler-Dealers is the time each waits for a pay-off and the follow-through necessary for that pay-off. Foresight—the ability to visualize long-range potential and work for deferred rewards—is fundamental to the Entrepreneur's success (and usually sorely lacking in Wheeler-Dealers). This is because most ventures take years to realize any profits.

Where Do I Start?

Virtually all Entrepreneurs "cut their teeth" in a corporate setting, as a Persuader or a Wheeler-Dealer. At some point—usually due in part to a stifling hierarchy—each of these Entrepreneurs, often with only the concept for a new enterprise, invested themselves and their savings in making that idea a reality.

Rather than using their persuasive talent to sell the company's goods and services, these Entrepreneurs embark on a mission, using their aptitudes and abilities to promote their own product or idea. Many Entrepreneurs exchange the short-term rewards and big commissions they could earn in the short run for visions of what the future holds. Their incentive becomes the hope they hold that their product or service will fly. A strong Foresight aptitude, while not augmenting their success in sales, becomes the bedrock of their entrepreneurial ventures.

Where Do I Get Ideas?

Natalie launched her business after ten years in the medical sales division of a large conglomerate. Like many individuals with strong Foresight aptitude, she had worried about controlling her future in such a large company. She might or might not get the promotions and transfers she wanted. There was always the possibility that management would reorganize things or sell her division to another company. She was in no position to influence such events.

Moreover, most of the ideas she had presented to her bosses never got off the ground. The company wanted nothing but sales from its marketing representatives. It deeply bothered Natalie that her future and ideas were controlled by someone other than herself.

Natalie applied her creative problem-solving abilities (Ideaphoria, Analytical, and Diagnostic aptitudes) when she perceived an opportunity with one of the local hospitals. One of the hospitals agreed to try some of her employer's new monitoring devices for premature infants. When Natalie made a follow-up call to see how the nursery staff liked the equipment, she identified the need that provided the inspiration for her enterprise.

Donning a mask and gown, she followed the head nurse into the nursery. The incredibly small size of the premature babies struck her, and she could see that the probes taped to the their bodies interfered with feeding and dressing activities. They were simply too big.

Driving home, ideas whirled through Natalie's mind as she considered the size problems of prematurely-born infants. They didn't make baby clothes that small. The carriers people used to cart their babies from place to place seemed terribly awkward for such small infants.

Natalie decided to investigate the possibilities suggested by her storm of ideas. She visited mothers and fathers of premature babies and read all the pertinent information about problems attributed to the size of these infants. The nurses and doctors at hospital nurseries told her their stories, too.

Armed with this information and the conviction that she had a money-making idea, Natalie paid a seamstress to make several styles of tiny baby clothes. She gave her doll-like samples to parents of newborn premature babies and asked them for feedback every week. Their criticism gave her ideas for different openings for the head, arms, and legs and for the positioning of various buttons and snaps.

Natalie discovered that parents, especially the fathers, felt better about their undersized babies when the baby clothes did not threaten to swallow the tiny ones. Natalie's baby clothes made a positive difference in the parents' emotions towards their new children and in the speed and convenience with which they could change their babies' clothes.

After making several modifications and checking parents' reaction, Natalie took most of her savings and began her career as a premature baby clothes entrepreneur. She used her sales experience to promote the line in a personal way. She used an advertising agency to gain exposure to a larger market.

Natalie consulted with a retired apparel manufacturing executive as her operations grew from cottage size to manufacturing company size. Analyzing new products and design improvements required part of her attention. Meeting with bankers and financial and accounting advisors demanded her time, too.

Natalie was personally involved in every facet of the business. She built an organization around the way she believed things should be done. It took three years for Natalie to build the company into a profitable concern and regard it as a stable basis for her future.

Not Just Another Wheeler-Dealer

Natalie's success as an entrepreneur took much long-er than the days or weeks involved in the Wheeler-Dealer's transactions. She had to firmly believe in the possibilities of a distant future and trade off the income from her previous job and the bulk of her savings for that uncertain future. For her, the potential reward outweighed any sacrifice.

Natalie differs from Wheeler-Dealers in another way. She spent years following through on her idea and brought many people into her organization to make her idea a reality. She had to deal not just with customers, but with production workers, office staff, financial and legal advisors, bankers, and advertising consultants.

This kind of follow-through required persistence as well as organizational skills. Natalie orchestrated the activi-ties of numerous other people over a period of years to achieve her success.

Most Wheeler-Dealers interact with other people for shorter lengths of time, and they do not juggle as many people at the same time. They are not really concerned with building a company. They are concerned with making a sale.

Another thing that distinguishes Natalie's experience from that of the Wheeler-Dealer is that she actually produced something that did not exist before. She brought her idea together with labor and materials and energy to create some-thing. Wheeler-Dealers simply expedite the process of moving ownership of products from one entity to another.

Breaking The Corporate Mold

A novel idea propelled Natalie into entrepreneurship. Failure to fit into conventional companies propels certain other Entrepreneurs at a faster rate. Many Entrepreneurs have found it difficult to climb the corporate ladder, and a good number have actually antagonized the powers-that-be in traditional companies.

These individuals might be eccentric types who simply rub mainstream, conservative managers in the corporate setting the wrong way.

Others are so focused on the objective to be accomplished that they ignore the corporate power struc-ture and accompanying political struggles that, to them, seem irrelevant to the job at hand.

All These Aptitudes and Nothing To Do

For the non-corporate person, entrepreneurship can also provide an escape from the one-dimensional jobs typical of many large companies. For the person who likes to wear many different hats, entrepreneurship is a viable alternative.

With a bias toward action and change, these individuals are stifled by the channeling so predominant in corporate life. Entrepreneurs, while actualizing their potential, can achieve the satisfaction of wearing all their potential hats. Ultimately, the economy and the society benefit from the Entrepreneur's new product or service—which may have never gotten off the drawing board in the corporate game.

Matt, a "too-many-aptitude" big company reject, illustrates this point vividly. His background typifies the person who enjoys wearing many hats. As a student, he learned most things quickly, but found them boring in a short period of time.

Matt changed his college major five times. First he was a foreign language major, and he quickly became fluent in five languages. But when he started his senior year, Matt discovered that he could get a Bachelor of Arts in mathematics by taking three more math courses. The various requirements of premed, physics, and engineering majors— all of which he had switched into at one time or another—had given Matt a major by default.

Matt took the path of least resistance and majored in math. He thought that, at this point, getting a college degree in *any*thing would show some progress. He took statistics courses to complete the requirements for a math degree and discovered that statistics knowledge could be applied to any number of subjects.

That pleased Matt. He could learn about something new each time he applied statistical techniques to a new subject. Matt earned a graduate degree in statistics and worked on many of his professors' consulting jobs. Before completing his doctorate, he took a research position with a pharmaceutical company.

The pharmaceutical company expected Matt to work with the scientists testing new drugs on animals and special human population groups. Matt did everything his bosses expected and more. His lunch hour discussions with scientists in other departments led to his participation in the actual development of new drugs.

Going far beyond the bounds of his actual job description, Matt began assisting the head of research and development in mapping out research programs, planning budgets, and setting up ways to measure the progress of each program.

When a group or department ran into a statistical obstacle, it tapped Matt for ideas on ways around it. He got to wear all kinds of hats and utilized most of his aptitudes.

Despite the good match between his special projects job and his aptitude profile, Matt realized a nasty fact after about five years on the job—his company rewarded mediocrity. The exceptionally talented research and development people got few promotions, and their raises came mostly from cost-of-living adjustments. Meanwhile, otherwise-average scientists who were politically savvy progressed rapidly into management roles, where salaries, bonuses and benefits far exceeded those given to nonmanagement scientists.

Three incidents motivated Matt to flee the company and start his own business. One was the promotion of a singularly ruthless man. Immediately preceding the culmination of several successful projects, this man secured a managerial position, then claimed credit for breakthroughs that had taken the research team years to achieve. He convinced management that he effected these accomplishments, then pulled strings to fire several of the men and women actually responsible for them.

A second incident was both hilarious and frightening to Matt. In a meeting with the company's CEO, Matt explained that while not all attempts at inventing a certain type of drug were successful, but that about one in 35 were, the CEO demanded to know why the company wasted its time with the first 34 tries.

"Let some other company absorb the cost until they get close to the 35th attempt," he said. "Then we'll have a greater probability of success." At first Matt was astonished at the man's ignorance of statistics. Then he had to leave the room so he could laugh without being seen. That night Matt woke up suddenly an hour or two after midnight. It was frightening, he decided, to work for a company whose chief executive had such limited understanding of how its products were developed...and no understanding at all of simple statistics!

The final event that steered Matt into entrepreneurship was a conference with his nominal boss. The boss told him that three of the other managers had complained about his collaboration with scientists in their departments. They felt that Matt had stepped into places he didn't belong. The lines of authority gave these three managers no formal control over Matt, and they felt Matt was undermining them and invading their territories. This attitude frustrated Matt, because he knew his efforts had resulted in tangible progress in their departments.

Realizing that he would have nothing but unbearably boring work if he were restricted to the job for which the company had originally hired him, Matt resigned. Matt had no clear idea about what he would do next, but he knew he couldn't continue with the company.

As he contemplated possibilities, he began thinking of the strengths and weaknesses of the company he'd left. One fact suddenly dawned on him—his old company's scientists lacked the physics and engineering knowledge essential for the development of new biotechnical products, an area of immense opportunity.

This weakness of his old employer was the door of opportunity for Matt. If he could assemble the right team of scientists and convince someone to fund the start-up, he could form his own biotechnology company. Matt lived off his savings for another eight months while he contacted biologists, chemists, physicists, and engineers in the morning and bankers, venture capitalists, and wealthy individual investors afternoons and evenings.

Some of them, of course, told Matt he was naive and a little crazy to even think about such an ambitious undertaking. Eventually, though, he assembled all the necessary money and scientific and technical talent to launch his enterprise. The new company gave him an arena large enough to exercise all his aptitudes and an opportunity to create reward structures for good research scientists and good managers.

Most of the managers at Matt's old company made disparaging remarks about "Uncle Matt's commune of whiz kids," but Matt believed he had the right people in place to achieve scientific and financial success.

Often it is a company like Matt's that gives us a completely new product or technology impossible to develop in an established company, where managers stake out their territories and avoid risks with any measurable chance of failure. Too-many-aptitude people like Matt can span the gap between seemingly divergent fields and become catalysts for finding revolutionary solutions to tough problems.

Matt's company is brand-new, but I suspect we'll all be using its innovative products very soon.

Can You Afford To Fail?

One danger Matt faced, along with every other Entrepreneur, is the absence of organizational insulation. A person in a large organization almost never makes a mistake that is fatal to the company. An army of staff and line managers provides advice and alters decisions. When a mistake does happen, there is usually enough money to fix it or forget it, from the corporate point of view.

Though some people might get booted out of the company or demoted, the company itself will inevitably survive. Most Entrepreneurs do not have the people or the money to cushion the effects of a bad decision. A single mistake can eliminate both the Entrepreneur and his company.

Can You Afford Success?

Other reasons for failure among Entrepreneurs, especially the ones with too many aptitudes, arise when their companies *succeed*.

Too-many-aptitude people like Matt are uniquely qualified for the start-up phase. Fledgling companies might never survive the first year or two if the Entrepreneur with multiple aptitudes could not participate in every aspect of the business. Scarce resources and the need to shape the company around the Entrepreneur's idea make this kind of participation an asset to the company. If things go well, the company grows.

But all-too-often, as success happens, the established business outgrows the too-many-aptitude Entrepreneur. The need for more formal procedures to control the day-to-day functioning militates against the Entrepreneur's want to be intimately involved in every facet of the business.

Too-many-aptitude people are rarely effective in ongoing administrative work. They are prone to change the way things are done when they see room for improvement. These constant changes become counterproductive when employees spend most of their time learning new procedures. Finding a less creative person with fewer aptitudes to function as a C.E.O. solves the problem for some Entrepreneurs.

If the successful Entrepreneur transfers responsibility and authority for operations to a suitable manager, the company stands a greater chance of focusing on its purpose and continuing its growth. The "ideal" manager's aptitudes include weak Ideaphoria and a Generalist frame of reference. Many Entrepreneurs are Specialists with strong Ideaphoria, eliminating them from management roles.

Kim is a Specialist with strong Ideaphoria aptitude, an Entrepreneur whose company outgrew its need for her numerous aptitudes.

Several years ago, Kim started a tutoring service for middle school and high school students. Her organization enjoyed outstanding success due to Kim's ability to create an effective learning and motivational system. After students from other cities began attending the summer programs at her center, Kim set up a franchising system to extend the program to other regions. She thought that the service should be uniform from one city to the next, so she stipulated in the contracts that the franchisees had to adhere strictly to her system.

As the number of franchises multiplied, Kim hired people to oversee their adherence to her system and to manage the company's finances. She appointed an operations officer and a financial officer whom she trusted. Then she took an unusual step. She stepped far enough away from her newly appointed officers to let them do their jobs.

Putting all or part of their companies in the hands of other people is a wrenching experience for most Entrepreneurs, almost like waving good-bye to their children as they go off to school for the first time. Kim felt a sense of loss as she transferred authority from herself to more narrowly-focused individuals, but that sense of loss was coupled with a feeling of freedom.

Kim chose the right people to operate her and mobilized her wide array of aptitudes around another (and completely different) venture. Given her success at knowing when to leave the companies she starts, I have no doubt she will wind up as "mother" to a number of successful ventures.

Take The Money And Run

Sometimes Entrepreneurs don't just turn over operations to employees—they sell the business outright and use the proceeds to start another company. When used adroitly, this strategy provides the Entrepreneur with increasingly high standards of living as well as interesting work.

A fascinating example is Patrick, who used part of the profit from the sale of his automobile maintenance shops to create a business that is both very similar and very different from his previous venture. The business he sold catered to owners of European luxury cars, offering them a great deal of upscale service. Plush waiting rooms, deferential mechanics and service advisors, and delivery of the cars to customers' homes were just a few of the amenities distinguishing Patrick's repair shops from gas stations and car dealers.

His idea was that owners of certain cars would pay premium prices for extra attention and detailed information about their cars. He implemented that idea by hiring people who knew about the cars and who knew how to communicate with the upper-middle-class customers. There's a certain sincerity about Patrick, and his face lights up when he talks about his business ventures:

> I had a new car dealer ask me to set up a shop in conjunction with his dealership. His idea was that he'd own part and I'd own part. That made me think I could set up and sell a bunch of these service centers in different cities. Instead of selling them off one at a time, I could sell off the whole chain for a bundle. And that's what I did. I lucked out on the timing, and I found some good business brokers to find a buyer.
>
> That's how I got the money to start my new business. It takes a lot more equipment but fewer employees than my first business. We rent out garage space and tools by the hour for do-it-yourselfers.
>
> These folks are just the opposite of the rich customers I used to have. They buy American or Japanese cars, and a lot of them buy used cars. They change their own oil and know how to fix most of the things that go wrong with their cars. Sometimes they can't afford a major repair, and they can't spread parts all over the apartment parking lot to do it themselves. So they come here.
>
> We've got a parts store adjoining every garage, and we make as much from part sales as we do from hourly garage rentals. A television reporter came by last week, and we got on one of the local channels in a special feature at the end of the 6 o'clock news. They talked about my old company, too. Yesterday a woman from one of the big radio networks called to see if I'd do an interview about car repairs on one of those consumer shows. I guess I'm Mr. Personality in the car repair business.

Like so many Entrepreneurs, Patrick has more aptitudes than the average person. His Structural Visualization and Analytical aptitudes are the same as those of engineers. His Ideaphoria and Diagnostic aptitudes are typical of lively teachers and communicators. His Perceptual Speed is typical of accountants and financial analysts. He arranges his work so that he can do all these jobs. Most positions in conventional companies would allow him only one of them.

Hold On...

As with all generalizations, the idea that an Entrepreneur must remove himself when his company achieves success does not fit every situation. Business journalists describe Sam Walton, who opened this chapter, as a notable exception to the rule.

Not a few Entrepreneurs adequately make the transition from creative whirlwinds to buttoned-down administrators and continue to successfully operate their companies. However, they are not usually the Entrepreneurs with "too many" aptitudes. Annette, an introverted Generalist whose only strong aptitude is Analytical ability, exemplifies this type of Entrepreneur.

Annette started a temporary placement agency for physicians soon after her father closed his medical practice. After fifteen years in a dead-end job with a major insurance company, Annette was moved to begin her business by a nagging desire to do something meaningful with her life.

She was prompted to begin her venture by her father's depression upon retirement. When she discovered her insurance company needed a doctor to review various claims, Annette convinced her father to work a couple of days a week evaluating these cases.

Some of the other retired doctors her father knew were also interested in part-time work, but they didn't know how to find it. Annette's idea began to take shape, and she began researching it. There were, she discovered, a lot of insurance companies, hospitals, and group practices who needed temporary or substitute doctors but didn't know where to find them. Annette's company would match them up.

Over seven years, the company has doubled its revenues every year. Annette feels no restlessness with her work, and she has no compulsion to change her business. Her aptitudes have outlets, and she has succeeded financially.

What's The Bottom Line?

If you are an Entrepreneur or hope to become one, evaluate your aptitudes before planning your strategy.

If you do not have a lot of aptitudes, try to select a product or service to complement the ones you *do* have.

If you have too many aptitudes, be prepared to cope with the fact that your enter-prise might evolve into a work environment unsuitable for your personal happiness.

Shocking as it may seem, the ultimate goal of most successful Entrepreneurs is *not* to make incredible amounts of money. They want to make their *ideas* successful. When I asked one Entrepreneur I had known for almost ten years what it was he sought from all his hard work, he summed it up rather ambiguously, "I want to do what I can do."

Today, after studying many Entrepreneurs, this answer is perfectly clear.

Entrepreneur Business Careers

A list of job titles similar to those in other chapters in this book would make no sense for Entrepreneurs—their "jobs" depend on what they create.

If you are interested in further reading about Entrepreneurs, I would suggest starting with "Stalking the Entrepreneur," by David E. Gumpert *(Harvard Business Review,* May/June, 1986). He reviews four excellent books on entrepreneurs and suggests fledgling entrepreneurs add works by Joseph Schumpeter, Benjamin Franklin, Machiavelli, and Alfred Sloan to their reading list.

I would also recommend **Your First Book of Wealth** by A. David Silver (also published by The Career Press). Silver is the author of many of the reference works on entrepreneurship and venture capital; this is his introduction to the entire concept for the neophyte.

Professional and Trade Groups

American Enterprise Association
American Entrepreneurs Association
Association of Collegiate Entrepreneurs
Association of Venture Founders
Center for Entrepreneurial Management
Inventrepreneurs' Forum

National Association of Black Women
Entrepreneurs
National Venture Capital Association
Women Entrepreneurs
Young Entrepreneurs Organization

Professional Reading

Black Entrepreneur
Entrepreneur
Inc.

Success
Venture

Strong Aptitudes

ANALYTICAL *A methodical type of problem-solving ability useful in organizing, coordinating, and planning*

DIAGNOSTIC *An intuitive type of problem-solving ability helpful in investigation and research*

MANY OTHERS, *depending on specialty*

Weak Reinforcing Aptitudes

MANY OR FEW, *depending on specialty*

Eleven

The
Consultants

Elizabeth began her career as a Consultant after a brief but eye-opening stint in production management. She presently works with a large consulting firm, where her combination of aptitudes has made her a very effective.

Elizabeth has highly-developed Analytical, Diagnostic, Perceptual Speed and Structural Visualization aptitudes, all of which contribute to her work performance. Her synopsis of her career is a very accurate job description for any of you contemplating a career as a Consultant:

> Consulting was a natural choice. I'm good at solving problems and analyzing data, and I'm good with people. I am very self-confident with excellent communication skills. Out-of-town travel and long hours don't bother me. I've got

an MBA, which most of the big consulting firms require their entry level consultants to have.

Working with the senior consultants and partners gives me experience in a more dynamic environment. I can concentrate on production and operations management, but approach it in a way that highlights my personality and aptitudes. If I decide to work for a manufacturing or production company in the future, I'll have the experience and broad exposure to go in at the top, not the bottom.

Consulting, like entrepreneurship and small business ownership, provides an excellent arena for business people with an overabundance of aptitudes. Like Entrepreneurs, many Consultants, after several years of "towing the corporate line," leave the routine for the variety consulting offers.

Elizabeth's initial experience in production management characterizes the fate of many Consultants who begin in a corporate setting. After obtaining an MBA from Carnegie-Mellon, she began working for a huge food processing conglomerate. When offered a fast-track position in manufacturing management, she jumped at the chance.

Their management training program included stints as line supervisor, assistant production planner, assistant quality assurance manager, and assistant inventory manager. She received rave reviews from all of her supervisors...and was miserable:

When I was moved to assist the production planner, I anticipated making bigger contributions to the company. The roadblock I ran into was that people at that level simply weren't interested in improvements. They had their own way of doing things, and they certainly weren't going to change them at the behest of a young upstart a few months out of college.

In this position and all the rest along my fast-track path, I wasn't going to be a boss. I was going to be an assistant. I would be learning the way things were done, not trying to make them better.

Apparently the only places in this company for problem solvers was at the bottom—on the production line—or at the top—with people who had at least ten years with the company. The route to the top suddenly went from a dream to sheer drudgery.

Elizabeth wisely exited this situation and began her career as a Consultant.

She has never looked back. Her brief tenure in the corporate setting convinced her that a career in middle management was not her niche—a conclusion drawn by the vast majority of Consultants.

Soup De Jour

Consultants can generally utilize a multiplicity of their aptitudes because different projects demand different abilities.

A management information systems consultant, for example, might draw on Structural Visualization, the three-dimensional thinking aptitude, when setting up a system for a home builder. Structural Visualization might be useless for that same consultant's insurance company client, but then Perceptual Speed, the paperwork aptitude, might prove invaluable.

The key for most Consultants is to develop an expertise founded on their strengths, usually by finding outlets for various aptitudes in a particular industry.

Consulting work in manufacturing, construction, production, fabrication, agricultural, scientific, and technical types of businesses, for example, would use Structural Visualization.

A Consultant for apparel merchandisers, furniture companies, or art businesses would benefit from strong Design Memory.

Associative Memory, which is helpful in learning foreign languages, would be an asset to a Consultant concerned with international trade or dealing with foreign clients. And so on.

Not all Consultants are gifted with a plethora of aptitudes. Some have very few. These Consultants likely entered the field due to their entrepreneurial independence and a desire to escape the corporate culture. Unable to work happily as part of a large organization, they choose consulting as their route to self-employment.

Mandatory Aptitudes

The essential facet of the Consultant profile is whether they are strong in Analytical and Diagnostic abilities. Regardless of how many or how few other aptitudes Consultants possess, talent in problem-solving is integral to their success.

This proficiency enables Consultants to assimilate relevant information from their clients into some kind of cohesive strategy. Having plotted a course of action, the Consultant can oversee the implementation until problems are resolved. In some situations, he may remain under contract to a company for some time, trouble-shooting various glitches that occur.

Despite the importance of having *both* problem-solving aptitudes, some Consultants are strong in only one. If this is you, you must learn to use the strength of one aptitude to compensate for the weakness of the other.

Developing A Checklist To Compensate

As a Consultant with a strong Analytical but weak Diagnostic aptitude, you should approach your problem solving in a deliberate, methodical manner. Most Consultants in this category develop a checklist that enables them to identify client needs quickly.

Without adopting such a methodical approach, you may get surprised from time to time—reading between the lines just is *not* your forte. Seldom will you find a client company completely focused on what their problems are. The client might assume that certain unstated wants or needs are obvious. Many things are not obvious to Consultants with limited Diagnostic aptitude—you may have difficulty discovering the client's true situation if it is not explicitly declared.

To compensate for your problems in this area, you will find that organizing and coordinating the activities required to solve the client's problem are much easier. Making a logical presentation of your research and enumerating the steps necessary to implement your recommendations are where you will excel.

Elementary, Dr. Watson

On the other hand, a Consultant with strong Diagnostic aptitude has more natural intuition, which makes troubleshooting relatively easy. But if you possess little Analytical aptitude, the planning and organizing aspects of the job will require more effort.

This kind of Consultant uses a "seat of the pants" approach at client interviews, asking incisive questions, gluing together pieces of seemingly scrambled information, and testing out the mental connections being formed.

Putting things in a step-by-step order when explaining how to implement his recommendations is difficult. Though this Consultant jumps to conclusions readily, he struggles to map the necessary procedures to achieve these ends.

Imposing a predescribed for-mat on the work to be done is vital to such a Consultant's survival.

Getting Started

Shortly after leaving the food processing conglomerate, Elizabeth began her career with a large consulting firm. With several specialized divisions, this company offered the diversity Elizabeth wanted. Her division creates a team each time a new project begins.

One advantage of this type of consulting firm is that Elizabeth will learn from many people. The tutoring she receives with each assignment is preparing her for the day when *she* will be the mentor.

Another advantage of such a firm is that it offers the security of a corporate track...often with*out* all the trappings. Elizabeth anticipates moving up to the senior consultant level in four years, to the managing consultant level within ten, and, eventually, hopes to become a partner. If her career at the consulting firm doesn't develop as she expects, her experience will qualify her for decision-making positions in industrial management.

Large consulting firms like Elizabeth's might have specialties in every field or just one. Better known consulting firms include Boston Consulting Group, Lester Knight, and Hay Associates. The largest national CPA firms have management advisory services (MAS) divisions that offer consulting services. Smaller consulting firms abound, usually specializing in a particular type of service or client.

The Lone-Wolf

For the individual who wants to be his own boss, consulting is a viable alternative. One-man consulting operations abound due to the relatively minor start-up costs involved. People with extensive experience in a certain industry often "hang a shingle," much like a beginning doctor or attorney.

These Consultants might be in their fifties, sixties, or even older and retired from their previous companies. A much smaller number of self-employed Consultants are younger men and women disaffected by their employers or simply desirous of independence.

The difficulty for younger ("upstart") Consultants is gaining the savvy requisite to prosperity in a field that virtually demands expertise. It isn't easy. Early years can be too lean to support a family. Given these parameters, many would-be young Consultants with a limited network of contacts begin their consulting enterprises on a part-time basis.

Paul, a human resources Consultant, has his own practice. When he was 42 years old, he resigned from his position as a labor relations specialist with a multinational electronics company. After interviewing for a similar position with several other companies, Paul began to think about becoming a consultant. It would give him the opportunity to solve human resource management problems without getting mired in the kind of bog he found at the electronics company.

His activity in professional organizations and his good name among employers in the region would be assets. He was old enough and experienced enough to be credible, and he liked the idea of working for himself. Here's what he has to say about his experience:

I like what I do. Solving the people problems in business has always interested me. Sometimes a company will call me just to represent them in negotiations with their union. When the negotiations are over, I'll tell management how they could avoid some of their problems in the future. Sometimes our discussion turns into another consulting project for me, one with a more strategic approach.

When I started my consulting practice, I underestimated the drastic changes in my lifestyle it would necessitate. We bought a bigger house so we could entertain clients in our home. I spend more money on clothes and restaurants.

I'm usually out of town to see a client eight or ten days each month. I have to bring in a lot more income and work longer hours than I anticipated to cover these expenses. A lot of them are tax-deductible, of course, but I still have to pay my own health insurance premiums and squirrel away some money for retirement. These things worry me sometimes, but I feel a lot freer as a consultant than I did as an employee. I like the freedom, and I like the work.

The High Price You'll Pay

Paul handles the demands of his consulting business well. He is healthy, and he thrives on the stress of meeting deadlines. But the long hours, frequent travel, and time pressure could well become obstacles for other Consultants, whether they are self-employed or working for large consulting firms. Seventy-hour work weeks and weekend work are par for the course. Being away from spouse, children, and friends on a regular basis is to be expected.

Some people yearn for the high income and prestige of consulting, but they cannot make the necessary sacrifices. Lack of physical stamina or a medical disability can preclude success, too. Refusing to give up leisure time and some family activities interferes with consulting careers for most people. If you think consulting is the career for you, carefully evaluate your tolerance for these working conditions.

Can You Schmooze?

Some would-be Consultants never get out of the starting gate because they lack the personal skills necessary for strong client relations. These Consultants fail for the same reasons as some of the Persuaders discussed in Chapter 3.

An absence of amiability undermines the success of some Consultants—especially Introverted Specialists who are severely limited in personal skills. Clients are put off by what they perceive as cold and aloof individuals.

There are two ways to deal with this problem. First, the introverted Specialist can gain such renown that the shortcomings of his personality are overlooked. Writing books or newsletters in his field of expertise, getting articles published in professional journals, and teaching graduate students at a university are ways a Consultant can get his name recognized. Getting the most highly-regarded professional certification in the consulting specialty bestows an additional credential.

The second approach for the introverted Specialist is to find an extroverted partner or associate to make the initial client contacts and keep interpersonal relationships with clients on a good footing. Quite a few introverted Specialists team with extroverted Generalists in establishing a consulting firm. If the Extrovert and the Introvert can achieve some sort of symbiosis, the relationship can be very prosperous.

A Ladder Not A Parachute

One unobtrusive pitfall for some Consultants is the absence of a clearly-defined career ladder—primarily true of those who place security at a high premium.

Kevin, an independent accounting and financial planning consultant, feels the lack of a career ladder acutely.

Shortly after he passed his CPA exams, he went to work for a large consulting firm and moved up the hierarchy at the expected pace. Before he became a partner, he struck out on his own. His annual income now exceeds $250,000, and there is always a new project or client waiting to pay for his services.

Kevin, it would seem, has made a more-than-successful transition to consulting. Nevertheless, he has nagging doubts about how well he's doing. His face is deeply lined and his brow is always furrowed. He explains his unsettled state this way:

> With my own consulting business, I don't have a clear-cut goal to work toward each year. I know I'm doing well financially, but I don't know how I compare with other people in my situation. Maybe I do a lot less than they do. It would be gratifying to know that I do a lot better. The goals I set for myself might be too high. Or maybe they're too low. I just don't know.
>
> The feedback I get is from my clients. Most of them are pleased with my work, and some of them express their appreciation for it. The trouble with this kind of thing is that it's not specific. Usually they don't tell you precisely what they think is good. And you certainly don't want to go out of your way to elicit negative comments from your clients. If you did a poor job, you don't want to remind them.

Kevin might have encountered similar frustration as a partner or director at his old consulting firm. His peers in that situation, however, might have provided the yardstick for measuring his own success that he seems to need.

Perhaps Kevin does not have the independence that seems to be second nature to most Consultants. His reliance on the opinions of others might indicate problems with his future as a Consultant.

Are You Ready?

Before *you* embark on a consulting career, seriously evaluate the issues discussed in this chapter, and make sure you come to terms with the implications of these concerns prior to your leap. Consider the following checklist and discuss it with your family and peers—and listen to their concerns, too!

Do not underestimate how indispensable a *strong Analytical or Diagnostic aptitude* is. Consultants solve problems, and these are problem-solving aptitudes.

It is crucial to *select a consulting area that fits your overall aptitude profile,* along with your specific interests and knowledge.

Most successful Consultants are adept at *people skills.* Are you?

Most consulting jobs demand *sacrifice.* Long hours and extensive travel are the norm, leaving little, if any, time for family and recreation.

Self-employed Consultants must bear the full cost of supporting their enterprise. They have to charge fees four to six times higher than what they would be paid per hour as an employee to cover office, administrative, insurance, retirement, and other costs.

Do you have the *ego* for it? The happiest Consultants are rather independent-minded and only remotely concerned with others' impressions.

Do you have the *savvy and expertise* for it? Consultants usually specialize according to a particular industry or a specific skill.

Consulting Specialties

Skill Specialties

Accounting

Arbitration

Automation

Communications

Corporate fitness or
   wellness

Demography

Employee assistance

Executive search

Financial planning

Foreign languages and
   cultures

General management and
   top-level decision making

Government regulations

Human resources

Importing/exporting

Industrial geography

Labor relations

Logistics

Management information
   systems

Marketing

Operations

Organizational devel-
   opment

Outplacement

Pensions and compensation

Personnel

Physical distribution

Product development

Product recalls

Production

Promotion and publicity

Risk management

Safety

Security

Special events

Strategic planning

Telecommunications

Training and development

Turnaround

Industry Specialties

Agriculture

Aviation

Banking

Biotechnology

Chemical

Construction

Electronics

Energy

Entertainment

Health care

Food processing

Hotel

Hospital

Insurance

International trade

Manufacturing

Medical

Real estate

Recreation

Restaurant

Retailing

Transporation

Wholesaling

Professional and Trade Groups

American Association of Professional
Consultants

Association of Executive Search
Consultants

Association of Management Consultants

Association of Management Consulting Firms

Association of Outplacement Consulting
Firms

Institute of Management Consultants

International Association for Financial
Planning

International Association of Merger and
Acquisition Consultants

International College of Real Estate
Consulting Professionals

National Association of Telemarketing
Consultants

Society of Risk Management Consultants

Strong
Aptitudes

ALL, ANY, OR NONE, *depending on the type of business*

Weak Reinforcing
Aptitudes

EXTROVERT *An outgoing, sociable, somewhat impulsive personality*

Twelve

The Small Business Owners

Do you have the aptitudes to run your own business? Whatever you *did* answer, you *should* have answered "Yes!" Because *what*ever your aptitudes, there is probably a business that fits them. The real issue is *identifying* the business that ideally fits your aptitude profile.

Construction and manufacturing, for example, could use Structural Visualization and Design Memory. Data processing and bookkeeping services use Perceptual Speed, the computational and clerical aptitude.

Owning and operating a music store or a sound recording studio could take advantage of strong Tonal Memory, Pitch Discrimination, and other musical aptitudes. Finger Dexterity or Instrument Dexterity could be used if you owned a dental laboratory, locksmith shop, or computer repair and maintenance service.

You will find an extensive list of aptitudes cross-referenced with particular businesses in Appendix Two (pp. 189—198). They will give you additional ideas about how to use your aptitudes in your own business.

If you have no discernible aptitudes, the possibility for business ownership and operation still exists. Shaping the business around your interests, thoroughly learning all its aspects, and applying consistent effort to its operation can compensate for any lack of aptitude.

Where Did Everybody Go?

Strangely enough, the person most likely to struggle as a Small Business Owner is the Extrovert. Quite characteristically, unless these individuals spend the majority of their time in people-oriented activities such as sales or promotion, they feel trapped by mundane, day-to-day business operations.

Typical Small Business Owners do not embark on crusades to gain acceptance for a new business idea, nor do they spend most of their time selling. They concentrate on *running* the business, either by delegating tasks or doing the work themselves—rather pedestrian functions for the Extrovert.

Dave, an extremely extroverted man who set up his own retail store, gave this account:

> I didn't realize it would be so lonely! I thought a sporting goods store would combine my outgoing personality and my interests in the outdoors and sports. In high school and college, I worked on Saturdays for my uncle at his sporting goods store and loved it.
>
> Well, I found out that when I did it six days a week, my outgoing personality didn't have that many people to go out to. Sure, it gets busy in here on Saturdays, and I really love it then; but every other day, all I see is five or six customers at a time...max. It's too quiet for me.
>
> I used to play golf every Saturday or take my son's Boy Scout troop camping for the weekend. My wife and I would get together with friends three or four nights a week. Now I have to be here instead—people shop nights and weekends.

Dave's mistake is a good warning for Extroverts thinking about owning and operating their own businesses, especially retail businesses. You need to be sure you are ready to devote your entire life to an endeavor that may involve an abundance of very tedious detail work.

Some owner-operated businesses are appropriate for the Extrovert, especially those that depend on heavy customer contact: Resorts, hotels, restaurants, schools, day care centers, retirement villages, and similar facilities cater to large groups of people and have working environments more stimulating to Extroverts.

Small Business Owners who run sales organizations and make numerous sales calls themselves benefit from being extroverted. If an Extrovert in a partnership takes on the selling and promotion responsibilities, while a more introverted partner handles the administrative and managerial jobs, things can work out quite well for both of them.

You're In The Driver's Seat

The primary function of the Small Business Owner—even if the has only a limited number of employees—is *managing*. More than anything else, this separates them from Wheeler-Dealers, Consultants, and Entrepreneurs. Small Business Owners work on budgets, plan procedures, make purchases, and gather the information they need to make decisions. They concern themselves with the ongoing viability of their businesses.

Wendy, an Ambivert who owns and operates a medical laboratory for physicians, typifies the Small Business Owner managing her enterprise. Her experience illustrates the uphill climb most Small Business Owners experience in the start-up phase of their operation. After five years working as a medical technologist, Wendy became the lab manager. She recounts her progress from lab manager to owner-operator:

> Managing the lab was far more fulfilling than running the tests I was trained to do. Our efficiency improved after I took charge, and our mistakes fell to almost zero. I think people felt better after I became manager, because I did all these little things to improve the efficiency of the lab.

But the idea of being independent appealed to me. I'd gone as far as I could go at the hospital. Why not set up my own medical lab for doctors and clinics? My first step was to see if I had any potential customers. It would be pretty dumb to give up my hospital job and put a lot of money into something people didn't need.

What I discovered excited me. The only competitor in town apparently had abused his captive market. The office managers at the clinics and the doctors' assistants I chatted with gave me some good reasons to go into business.

I found out that they waited longer for test results than they used to and that prices had gone up a lot. The lab regularly sent test results to the wrong doctors. When time was critical or when they suspected a serious illness, many physicians put their patients in the hospital for some of the tests they could have done in the office. They just didn't feel they could rely on this outside lab.

My next step was to convince a bank to loan me some money to start up the lab. I showed them projected costs and expected revenues. My list of equipment was very detailed, and I made conservative assumptions about my ability to attract customers. The bank turned me down.

Maybe I didn't come across as strongly as I should have when I talked to them. Anyway, I enlisted some help from five doctors who really wanted another lab in town. They had their offices write some letters attesting to the fact that another lab was needed and asserting their intention to use my lab for their tests.

The first bank turned me down again, even after I showed them the five letters. I found out that three of my five supportive doctors used another bank, so I applied for a loan there. It came through.

Things were bumpy at first. I began to wonder if I'd done the right thing. I had not realized how much work it took to start up a business. I did so many things myself because I couldn't afford to hire more people. I'm glad I didn't give up because things are fine now. I like to make things tick. I like my independence. My laboratory has an outstanding reputation, and it's because I'm good at running it.

Wendy's progression is not uncommon among Small Business Owners—in fact, most of them recount similar trials and detours along their road to independence. The particular steps Wendy took provide a map through this start-up phase:

First, identify if there is a customer base that will support your business.

Second, amass the capital necessary to cover your start-up coats—for most would-be owner-operators, this can be their downfall. Few people realize the expense involved in establishing a business and keeping it running long enough to make a profit...*any* profit.

Finally, be mentally prepared for the bumps, lumps, and doubts that come with the long hours and sacrifices any infant business requires.

Aptitudes That Made It Happen

The aptitudes that Wendy utilized are indicative of the profile that best suits the Small Business Owner.

She is a Generalist and an Ambivert—a combination that helped make her be an effective lab manager, both at the hospital and in the initial phase of her own lab. These qualities continue to be invaluable assets in her business. Being on the same "wave length" with most people enables her to empathize with her customer base and suppliers.

Another component of Wendy's aptitude profile is her strong Analytical talent, which she used to find ways to increase efficiency at the hospital and when collecting information and organizing a business plan to present to bankers. Today her organizational skill enhances the day-to-day operation of her medical laboratory.

Wendy's weak aptitudes have also contributed to her success. For example, she lacks Ideaphoria. But in her training and early years as a medical technologist, in her managerial role at the hospital, and in her own business, Wendy has had no *need* for this aptitude.

In fact, strong Ideaphoria could have interfered with her success. The growth of her business depended on efficient operation and reliable service, not the promotion of something "new and improved."

All These Ideas And Nothing To Do

The emphasis on managing rather than promoting is why *weak* Ideaphoria is preferable for many Small Business Owners.

Weak Ideaphoria distinguishes many Small Business Owners from the Wheeler-Dealers and the Entrepreneurs. Strong Ideaphoria among Wheeler-Dealers and Entrepreneurs manifests itself in obvious ways. The Entrepreneur's new idea might seem offbeat to most of us—until he becomes a millionaire with that weird idea. Until then, he or she spends vast amounts of time and energy persuading investors and customers that coming from left field makes sense.

Most Small Business Owners do not need charisma, flair, or strong Ideaphoria to succeed—unlike the Entrepreneur or Wheeler Dealer who relies on hispersonality so much. When Small Business Owners *do* have strong Ideaphoria, they are likely to use it in ways that do not draw attention to themselves.

If outside sales is essential to the success of the company, the Small Business Owners with strong Ideaphoria are likely to spend time calling on customers. Some businesses, such as catering and party planning, benefit from fresh ideas on a regular basis, and the Ideaphoria aptitude could help.

Larry, who owns a chain of auto supply stores says the variety in his work keeps his strong Ideaphoria from being a problem:

> I don't get bored because I get to do a little bit of everything. Sure, I spend some time in meetings with the money and legal guys, but that's only a part of what I do. I keep up with what the computer geniuses are doing for our inventory and bookkeeping systems.
>
> I stay up-to-date on the products hitting the market. My visits to the stores tell me a lot about how things are going, and they're fun. I have a good rapport with my managers, so we talk about other things when the business is done.
>
> I appear in some of the television commercials we do, and that's a blast. My ad-libs have stayed in a lot of them because they come off better than the lines I was supposed to say. I don't think my work is creative, but the variety stimulates me. I like not doing the same things every day.

Delegate The "Dirty" Work

One incentive for being a Small Business Owner is the authority to delegate those jobs you don't like or don't do well —allowing you to concentrate on the things that are more fun. Of course, you must achieve a level of success that affords you this luxury, a goal of most owner-operators.

Attaining this freedom from the menial and distasteful duties motivates typical Small Business Owners— especially during the early stages when they must perform such "gopher work." Once they have reached their goal, they can mold their work around their preferences and talents.

One boutique owner, an introverted Specialist with strong Ideaphoria and Design Memory aptitudes, hired a Generalist who was an Ambivert as a manager when she expanded to additional locations. The manager did not have the owner's creative and design aptitudes. This arrangement allowed the owner to spend more time doing art work for advertisements and creating new specialty items for the store. The upscale and rather quaint image derived from these efforts gave her boutiques their reason for being.

Small Business Owners might spend their first few years sweeping the floors and keeping the books, as well as doing every other job to keep their businesses afloat. But eventually most create jobs for a number of other people— even Small Business Owners with multiple aptitudes find it impossible to do *every* job in a growing business.

A Niche For The Untalented

Most of the Small Business Owners discussed to this point have had strong aptitudes in at least one or two areas. There are a number of Small Business Owners who have no apparent natural ability in problem solving (Analytical and Diagnostic aptitudes), creativity (Ideaphoria), three-dimensional thinking (Structural Visualization), dexterities, paperwork aptitude (Perceptual Speed), or any other area. But they *still* succeed!

Their secret is that they took the time to learn a particular business thoroughly before launching their own.

They made up for their lack of natural ability with experience and hard work. (Small Business Owners with stronger aptitudes spend less time training and acquiring experience, although they too fare better, of course, with a solid knowledge of the businesses they choose to own.)

Sean, the prosperous owner of a wholesale nursery, has no strong aptitude beyond his Generalist and Introvert qualities. At the end of his five years in college, he had a degree in agribusiness and a good basic grasp of business concepts and practices in agriculture. While in school, Sean spent his summers working for a large wholesale nursery, where he gained supervisory status.

Upon graduation, he began working for a small nursery, a sole proprietorship. The owner had no children and had recently suffered a heart attack. To ease his stress and to keep his business viable, this man hired Sean to be his right hand—a logical choice because of Sean's degree and experience.

Sean's boss taught him every aspect of the business. Within two years, Sean had assumed full responsibility for operating the nursery whenever the owner took extended vacations. As Sean became more competent, his boss spent more time away.

Shortly after Sean's thirty-second birthday, the owner died. A few months later, Sean approached the widow about buying the business. She sold it to him and agreed to be paid in installments over a period of ten years.

Sean has thrived...despite his lack of aptitudes. The right training situation combined with his diligent effort prepared him to be a Small Business Owner.

The McDonald's Way

Franchising can be another option for would-be Small Business Owners who have a dearth of aptitudes or lack relevant experience. Most new franchisees have never operated their own businesses. The franchisers participate with the franchisee in selecting a location; help them design the facility and set up the books; show them how to hire, train, and fire employees; and give advice on marketing and running the operation.

The franchisee might benefit from the quantity discounts and lower prices due to the centralized purchasing power of the franchiser. He might draw more customers with extensive advertising and promotion campaigns that he could not afford on his own.

The drawbacks to buying a franchise include less independence and higher start-up costs than other Small Business Owners. Franchise contracts specify standard policies that franchisees must follow. If the franchisee fails to adhere to them, the franchiser can terminate the contract.

People who like to be innovative or do things differently might not like being franchisees. Buying a franchise involves an up-front fee that might range anywhere from a few thousand dollars to a million dollars or more. Then the franchisee pays royalties on his gross sales. He might pay for the building, land, and equipment he leases from the franchiser. He might pay even more money for goodwill or a special location.

As a general rule, it costs *less* to buy a franchise providing business and personal services like accounting, tax preparation, and employment placement. It costs *more* to buy one that requires a lot of equipment—a hotel, restaurant, or convenience store, for example.

Regardless of how much they pay for their franchises, all franchisees depend on the good business sense and good conduct of their franchisers. If the franchiser makes incorrect assumptions about consumer behavior and economic trends, the franchisees suffer.

Not all franchisers are ethical. Some have been known to divert the franchisees' advertising fees into general operating funds or to sell used equipment to franchise buyers at new equipment prices.

To avoid unscrupulous franchisers, it is essential to investigate them thoroughly. The Federal Trade Commission requires franchisers to furnish disclosure documents to prospective franchisees. Many states require registration of franchisers. Regulators look at their audited financial statements, details of the franchising arrangement, names and addresses of at least ten franchisees, and any litigation and bankruptcy proceedings.

If you think you want to buy a franchise, take these steps:

First, analyze your abilities and interests. Consider what you do well and what you like to do.

Second, consult a directory of franchisers to see what the possibilities are. Franchise Opportunities Handbook, compiled by the United States Department of Commerce, lists more than a thousand franchise companies and gives details on how they operate and how much their franchises cost.

After seeing what is available, write the companies that interest you and ask for names of franchisees that you can contact. Then talk to these franchisees about their businesses—they can give you a realistic idea about what it would be like owning a franchise like theirs.

Finally, see a lawyer and an accountant. Have them go over the contract with you line by line. You should understand every detail. They should review all disclosure documents required by the Federal Trade Commission and the state. Franchise agreements usually last 10 to 20 years. You should know as much as possible about the franchiser and exactly what your agreement is before you sign a contract.

Doubles Anyone?

Another route to business ownership for those lacking the aptitudes, the experience, or the capital is to find one or more partners. Sometimes partners provide the money to start the business, but take no active role in its operation. In other cases, all the partners contribute start-up capital to the business and all of them work in it to some degree.

Too often, the dream of having a stake in your own business gets you into a bad partnership arrangement.

Be careful. Taking on a partner is very much like being married. When the parties involved do not clearly define—preferably in writing—their respective roles, trouble soon follows.

A woman who owned half of a janitorial service company described her partner this way:

> The original idea was that she would do quality checks on our cleaning crews, make sure they had adequate supplies, and coach them on improvement when they made mistakes. I would do all the sales to prospective customers and negotiate with the banks.
>
> Well, I saw the customers and brought in the business, and now they call me, not her, when they're not happy. All she does is the office work, things we could hire a secretary to do. The cleaning crews hassle me when they need equipment or supplies. She should stay on top of things like that so they don't run out. We wouldn't have so many customer complaints if she'd do her part of the work.
>
> I think I got screwed.

Like too many business partners, these two failed to put into writing their respective roles and responsibilities in the emerging company. If you are planning to enter a partnership—even if your prospective partner is your best friend —write a job description for yourself and for each partner.

Once this is completed, meet and compare notes *before* you borrow or invest money or make legal contracts. After such an exercise, decide if this partnership is what you really want—with your eyes wide open. If it is, all partners will have written documents as references and reminders of their duties.

Not Much Margin For Error

In a large company, employees have "organizational insulation." They can draw on the knowledge of their fellow workers and win the approval of their bosses before they take action. If the action is a mistake, the big company usually has the financial power to absorb it.

Obviously, this is a different world than that of the Small Business Owner! The luxury of making mistakes— whether from ignorance or just making a bad decision—is available only to the most well-financed owner/operator. For the typical Small Business Owner—who has mortgaged his life to make his business fly—mistakes can have devastatingly tragic consequences.

Amy suffered the consequences of her ignorance when she started a day care center for preschoolers. A vivacious woman, she had been a kindergarten teacher in a public school system for ten years.

Her business suited her aptitudes, her experience, and her interests. An extroverted Specialist with extremely strong musical aptitudes, she wanted to make music a bigger part of the children's lives. Combining the day care concept with enriching music activities, Amy hoped to achieve that goal and develop a business of her own in the process.

She put together an impressive business plan, which, combined with the great demand for child care in her area, easily earned her a loan from the local bank. Amy found the right building, and she hired wonderful people to assist her. She found good deals on equipment and supplies.

A newspaper story brought in hundreds of interested parents, many of whom enrolled their children. Unfortunately, this publicity also caught the eye of a government official who wondered if Amy had the necessary state license.

The state licensing agency had recently decided to crack down on unlicensed day care centers. This official decided that some publicity about enforcement of the licensing requirement would serve as a warning to others.

Like some of the others, Amy was unaware of the legal requirement for a license. *Un*like the others, she was used as an example of what can happen when a day care center does not have one. The state agency slapped an exorbitant fine on her, costing her tremendous expense in legal fees and fines. To survive, she was forced to mortgage her house, sell one of the family cars, and work without salary for two years. Amy saved her business, but she paid dearly for her ignorance.

An Ounce Of Prevention

The best way to avoid a mistake like Amy's is to work for someone else who already owns the type of business you would like to own. Select a company small enough to give you a comprehensive view of the entire operation, as well as the essential financial and legal picture.

Working for too large a company can give you thorough training in the part of the company where you work but leave you ignorant about the way the rest of the business works. You might have too specialized a viewpoint when you leave, and your narrow focus could be your undoing as a Small Business Owner.

Stick To The Knitting

Some Small Business Owners founder because they fail to keep their businesses focused on the product or service on which they were started. After achieving a measure of success, some unrelated opportunity pops up and seems to offer a new way for the business to make more money.

A retailer, for example, could be approached by wholesalers with products that do not fit the store's purpose or image. The clients of a service business could suggest additional things the business was not originally designed to do. Sometimes these changes make sense; more often they don't.

If the small business offers disparate products or services, it betrays its niche. Customers, and even the Small Business Owner himself, become confused about what kind of business it really is. Customers start wondering if the owner is really serious about what he does. Offering products or services that are too diverse quickly uses up resources that could have been spent building and stabilizing a specialized niche.

If you plan to own your own business, define your niche and fight off any temptation to venture into tangential areas. "Dance with them that brung ya" and "stick to the knitting" are cliches you should take to heart. If you choose to diversify, be sure it is a strategic step, not an infatuated whim.

Do Not Underestimate The Costs

Most experts agree that the primary reason for small business failure is inadequate capitalization—underestimating the money needed to establish and keep a business going.

Such collapses occur when owners are too optimistic about the company's revenues, too sloppy predicting costs, or hesitant or unable to acquire more capital than originally anticipated.

Make sure to thoroughly investigate the costs of equipment, facilities, supplies, employees, and other overhead items. Have a detailed business plan with a clear explanation of what you plan to do, as well as projected revenues and expenses. Taking these precautionary steps before seeking capital can only aid you as you approach banks, private investors, silent partners, or your own bank account for an influx of money.

Satisfaction Guaranteed

Operating your own business has its perils, but the satisfaction of being your own boss and the absence of a ceiling on your income are two very real rewards.

In addition to these, you will find that as you grow older and richer, your business can provide you with the priceless opportunity to shape your work around your personal needs, interests, and aptitudes.

In Appendix Two, I've listed hundreds of small businesses that use various aptitudes and combinations of aptitudes. Keep in mind that the aptitudes specified in the headings are not *necessary* for success in the small businesses listed under it, but those small businesses would give you the greatest *opportunity* to use those aptitudes.

Most people become dissatisfied when they become bored with their work, and neglecting to use strong talent is one reason for boredom.

Few people get bored with their work if they like it and find it challenging, even when they do not have the full complement of useful aptitudes.

Even if you do not have all the aptitudes for a particular kind of business, you could still become successful at it!

Professional and Trade Groups

American Federation of Small Business
American Franchise Association
Center for Family Business
Chamber of Commerce of the United States
International Council for Small Business
International Franchise Association
National Association for the Self-Employed

National Association of Private Enterprise
National Association of Women Business
  Owners
National Family Business Association
National Small Business Administration
Small Business Administration
Small Business Assistance Center

Professional Reading

Franchise
Franchising World
In Business

Inc.
Success
Venture

Appendix One

A Summary Of Aptitude Characteristics

Generalist

Sees things as most people do

Understands the actions/reactions of others most of the time

Functions well as team member

Performs well in jobs requiring a little knowledge about a lot of things

Goes along to get along

Can "wing it" dealing with people in an organizational structure

Emphasizes interpersonal skills

Specialist

Has a subjective outlook

Often misinterprets the actions/reactions of other people

Finds it difficult to compromise

Performs well in jobs requiring deep knowledge of narrow area

Casts the one dissenting vote in an election

Needs well-delineated lines of authority in an organizational structure

Emphasizes personal competence

Extrovert

Acts before thinking
Talks a lot
Goes out a lot
Plays practical jokes
Moves quickly
Likes a lot of people around
Has a wide circle of
acquaintances
Thinks out loud

Introvert

Stops and thinks before acting
Does not talk much until well
acquainted with another person
Is more likely to be shy
Likes quiet surroundings
Keeps feelings under control
Moves in slow and unhurried
manner
Has few but special friends
Places great value on ethical
standards

Ambivert

Enjoys contact with people, but
not very aggressive contact
Can be content spending more
time alone than the Extrovert
Does not exhibit extremes in the
pace of physical movement
Is neither overly impulsive nor
very introspective

Is effective in jobs that require
both solitary work and contact
with people
Sometimes acts 100% extroverted; sometimes 100%
introverted

Strong Ideaphoria

Has very short attention span
Daydreams a lot
Can think of examples to illus-
trate a point very quickly
Talks a lot
Cannot concentrate on detailed
work for long periods
Has unusually low tolerance
for routine or repetitive jobs and
makes more mistakes than
other people in these types of jobs
Functions best in creative and
imaginative jobs
Needs more variety than others
Has trouble sticking to the
subject in meetings

Weak Ideaphoria

Can concentrate for long
periods of time
Takes consistent approach to
ongoing administrative tasks
Has difficulty brainstorming
Takes "no nonsense" approach
to problems
Finds it difficult to give extem-
poraneous talks

Makes fewer mistakes on routine or repetitive jobs

Sticks to the subject in meetings

Strong Analytical

Takes deliberate and methodical approach solving problems

Easily sees how particular items fit into an overall scheme

Can function with a messy desk or disorganized physical surroundings and remember where things are

Categorizes things quickly

Finds it easy to plan and organize ideas or activities

Weak Analytical

Spends more time on planning, scheduling, and coordinating ideas and activities

Has difficulty solving a complicated problem by breaking it into series of smaller problems

Takes longer to put ideas into a logical order

Needs organized environment to find things easily

Spends more than average amount of time making an outline or flow chart

Strong Diagnostic

Can debate either side of issue

Says "Yes, but..." a lot

Postpones making decisions because all advantages and all disadvantages are apparent

Can find something wrong with anything

Has very little patience with people in situations that require "hand holding"

Talks himself out of a lot of things

Sees the answer to problem before going through steps to solve it

Has thought about being a lawyer at one time or another

Weak Diagnostic

Does not argue for the sale of arguing

Makes very few sarcastic remarks

Has patient, accepting attitude when dealing with other people

Needs more explanation and examples when learning a new concept

Needs "devil's advocate" when weighing pros and cons to make a decision

Appears more decisive to others

Strong Foresight

Did not frequently change majors in college

Has graduate/professional degree

Prefers a small company to a large one

Is motivated when rewards are far in the future

Considers long-term consequences when considering a course of action

Finds it easier to endure lean years when starting a business

Needs long-range goals in addition to short-range goals

Weak Foresight

Needs frequent feedback on performance

Is highly motivated by immediate rewards

Changes long-range plans frequently

Changed college major several times

Must put extra effort into making and sticking to strategic plans

Achieves a long-term goal by setting a series of short-term goals leading to it

Gives up on long-range goals before they have had time to be achieved

Strong Perceptual Speed

Produces great amounts of paperwork in short periods of time with very few mistakes

Completes long written tests with time to spare

Fills out order forms and routine reports quickly

Feels comfortable at a desk doing pencil-and-paper work

Does not routinely transpose numbers or letters

Finds mistakes quickly when checking details in reports or calculations

Weak Perceptual Speed

Transposes numbers or letters frequently

Has trouble completing objective tests within a time limit

Make clerical and computational mistakes when pushed for speed

Loses his place on computer-graded answer sheets

Is among the last in the class to finish written work

Produces accurate paperwork... slowly

Strong Structural Visualization

Can quickly learn to read blueprints, contour maps, x-rays

Needs results that are tangible
or that can be quantified

Can visualize how an object
will look before the object
actually exists

Has mother or grandparent in
"structural" occupation such as
medicine, engineering,
science, or art

Is restless when working only
on ideas that have no basis in
physical reality

Can visualize three-dimensional structures in his mind
that he cannot see with his eyes

Weak Structural Visualization

Had problems with advanced
college courses in architecture,
engineering, or science

Must see an object or a three-
dimensional model of it to
know how it really looks

Spends more time learning to
interpret blueprints, contour
maps, and x-rays

Finds pleasure in working with
ideas or people, even when there
are no measurable results

Strong Associative Memory

Can quickly and accurately
memorize foreign language
vocabulary

Remembers technical or
specialized words easily

Makes good grades in courses
emphasizing knowledge of
particular subject's jargon

Weak Associative Memory

Must drill consistently to
memorize a foreign language
vocabulary in print

Cannot cram before a test to
remember a specialized or
technical vocabulary

Must reinforce memory of
foreign language, specialized,
or technical words by saying,
hearing, and writing them

Strong Design Memory

Can accurately remember and
duplicate a briefly-seen design

Remembers design features of a
piece of clothing or furniture

Good grades in art history,
electronics, anatomy courses

Weak Design Memory

Must make a sketch or drawing for later reference to remember design features

Cannot recall differences in design details of clothing, furniture, and art objects

Spends extra time studying for art appreciation courses

Strong Number Memory

Remembers telephone numbers easily

Recalls prices of the same item at different stores when doing comparative shopping

Works with reams of financial data but can recall important dollar figures without looking them up

Knows bank account, insurance policy, social security, and many phone numbers by heart

Weak Number Memory

Looks up frequently-used numbers

Sometimes forgets his own driver's license and social security numbers

Must write down important numbers

Strong Finger Dexterity

Can type and operate a calculator quickly

Handles laboratory equipment deftly

Easily connects jewelry clasps

Easily manipulates buttons and lenses on cameras

Can quickly and accurately assemble objects with very small parts

Weak Finger Dexterity

Drops dishes and kitchen utensils frequently

Punches the wrong buttons on telephones, calculators, control panels, and other equipment

Takes longer to complete art and craft projects, such as modeling with clay, origami

Strong Instrument Dexterity

Can perform repair jobs quickly with small tools

Adept at using tweezers, small brushes, paring knives, needles, and drafting instruments

Works quickly at electronics assembly

Weak Instrument Dexterity

Has great difficulty manipulating delicate objects with small tools

Botches repair jobs using small pliers, tweezers, needles, and similar tools

Takes longer to complete art and craft projects such as knitting, needlepoint, sewing

Strong Pitch Discrimination

Sings on key

Can tune a guitar

Can focus a camera quickly

Perceives tiny differences in things with sense of sight, touch, or hearing

Weak Pitch Discrimination

Sings off key

Takes a long time to focus a camera

Must put extra time into precision work

Has trouble perceiving small differences in light and texture

Strong Tonal Memory

Can accurately hum or sing a tune after hearing it once

Plays instruments by ear

Recalls melodies easily

Weak Tonal Memory

Must read music to play an instrument

Cannot remember tunes

Must hear a melody several times before remembering it

Strong Time Discrimination

Can sense tempo and repetitious patterns of sound

Can catch or hit a ball easily

Weak Time Discrimination

Cannot stay on a beat

Has trouble hitting a moving target

Strong Rhythm Memory

Can remember complicated rhythm patterns

Taps out rhythm patterns with a pencil without being aware of it

Has well coordinated movements for dance and sport

Weak Rhythm Memory

Takes longer to learn new dance steps

Requires longer hours of practice for skillful sports performance

Forgets complicated rhythm patterns

Strong Timbre Discrimination

Has good voice for singing solos but trouble blending with a choral group

Can modulate speaking voice to sound pleasing to other people

Enjoys saxophone or other rich-sounding instrument

Weak Timbre Discrimination

Blends voice with a choral group well

Must work to develop a good speaking voice

Performs better with a flute or other pure-sounding instrument

Strong Loudness Discrimination

Can balance speakers on a stereo easily

Notices slight variations in loudness when listening to radio and television programs

Plays piano with attention to fortissimo and pianissimo

Weak Loudness Discrimination

Must use meters or digital readouts to adjust sound equipment

Does not notice nuances of softness and loudness when listening to classical music

Appendix Two

Potential Small Businesses For Particular Combinations Of Aptitudes

Analytical Aptitude

Accounting and bookkeeping machines and supplies wholesaling or retailing

Butler and maid agency

Chauffeur and limousine service

Circular and sample distribution service

Data processing equipment wholesaling or retailing

Delivery service

Garbage collection service

Meetings and facilities coordination service

Moving service

Packing and crating service

Parking facility

Analytical & Diagnostic Aptitudes

Drug or alcohol abuse treatment center

Editing and rewriting service

Publishing

Repossessing service

Resume writing and preparation service

Security guard and patrol service

Design Memory

Advertising specialties supply

Antiques

Apparel wholesaling or retailing

Architectural supply

Art and crafts supplies

Art gallery

Awning, tent, or canopy wholesaling or retailing

Bridal shop

Building material wholesaling or retailing

Cards and gifts wholesaling or retailing

Carpet and rug wholesaling or retailing

China and flatware wholesaling or retailing

Church furnishings supply

Dancing supply

Fabric wholesaling or retailing

Flag and banner supply

Fur wholesaling or retailing

Home furnishings wholesaling or retailing

Jewelry wholesaling or retailing

Leather goods wholesaling or retailing

Lighting fixture wholesaling or retailing

Optical dispensary

Photography studio

Shoe wholesaling or retailing

Wall coverings wholesaling or retailing

Design Memory & Analytical Aptitude

Aerial photography service

Business forms design and production

Catalog designing and compiling service

Costume rental

Drafting and design technology service

Electronics design and production

Formal wear rental

Graphic arts production

Legal graphics service

Printing

Design Memory, Analytical Aptitude & Ideaphoria

Graphic or advertising design service

Greeting card design and production

Grooming, color, and image improvement service

Package design service

Window dressing and merchandise display service

Design Memory & Dexterities

Automobile customizing service
Blueprinting service
Bookbinding service
Custom tailoring service
Dental laboratory
Dog and cat grooming service
Drapery fabrication and installation service
Electrical installation and repair service
Florist
Furniture or antique restoration and repair service

Gift wrapping service
Gourmet shop
Interior plant leasing and maintenance
Make-up and hairdressing service
Motion picture processing laboratory
Nursery or greenhouse
Photographic processing laboratory
Sign fabrication and installation
Taxidermy service

Dexterities

Amusement equipment repair and maintenance service
Appliance repair service
Automobile detail and clean-up service
Automobile repair and maintenance service
Bakery
Beverage equipment repair service
Bicycle dealership
Building exterior cleaning service
Carpet and rug cleaning service
Carpet laying service
Chimney cleaning service
Computer repair and maintenance service
Copying and duplicating service
Dry cleaning equipment repair service
Electrical installation and repair service
Electrolysis clinic
Fence installation service
Flag pole installation service
Furniture cleaning service

Janitorial and general cleaning service
Lawn installation and maintenance service
Leather repair service
Locks and security devices installation and repair service
Microfilming service
Mobile home and portable building repair service
Office machine repair service
Painting contracting
Parking area maintenance and marking service
Pest control service
Radio and television repair service
Reweaving service
Roofing installation and repair service
Swimming pool service
Vending machine repair and maintenance service
Window cleaning service

Dexterities, Analytical & Diagnostic Aptitudes

Art school
Cooking school
Funeral home and mortuary

Medical laboratory
Riding academy
Testing laboratory

Dexterities, Analytical Aptitude & Perceptual Speed

Analytical laboratory
Court reporting training service

Dry cleaning and laundry service
Home nursing service

Diagnostic Aptitude

Detective or investigative agency
Dispute mediation service
Information research service

Insurance investigation service
Personal shopping service

Extroverted Personality

Amusement park
Camp
Dude ranch
Health and fitness club

Night club
Race track
Recreational facility
Skating rink

Extroverted Personality, Ideaphoria, & Analytical and/or Diagnostic Aptitude

Catering service
Class reunion planning service
Convention and trade show planning service
Day care center

Entertainment productions and services
Executive etiquette training service
Hotel
Modeling agency

Party planning service
Publicity service
Resort
Restaurant

Retirement village
Talent agency
Tour service
Wedding planning service

Extroverted Personality, Ideaphoria & Perceptual Speed

Apartment leasing service
Automobile dealership

Insurance agency
Boat dealership

Ideaphoria, Analytical & Diagnostic Aptitudes

Acting school
Children's and teen-agers' etiquette school
Children's home
Corporate history service
Literary agency
Maternity home

Modeling school
Montessori school
Motivational and self-improvement program service
Real estate school
Writing service

Music Aptitudes

Background music service
Band instrument supply
Dance school or studio
Mobile DJ and party music service
Music box exchange
Music instruction service
Musical instrument supply

Piano and/or organ tuning service
Radio program production
Radio station
Sound recording studio
Stereophonic and high fidelity equipment wholesaling or retailing

Music Aptitudes & Design Memory

Audio-visual equipment wholesaling or retailing

Audio-visual production service

Motion picture production service

Multimedia production service

Professional concert and theatrical equipment service

Sound system design

Television station

Theater

Video production service

Music Aptitudes, Perceptual Speed & Analytical Aptitude

Audio-visual equipment rental

Booking agency for musicians

Industrial sound level testing service

Orchestra agency

Record, tape, and sheet music wholesaling or retailing

Perceptual Speed

Billing service

Bookkeeping service

Check cashing service

Data processing service

Insurance billing and claims service

Mailing service

Payroll service

Secretarial service

Ticket agency

Word processing and typing service

Perceptual Speed & Analytical Aptitude

Accounting service

Appraisal service

Automobile parts wholesaling and retailing

Automobile renting and leasing

Book wholesaling or retailing

Business forms and systems service

Computer programming and software design service

Courier service

Credit reporting agency

Department store

Directory and guide publishing

Employment agency

Filing equipment and systems wholesaling or retailing
Freight forwarding service
Grocery store
Hardware store
Household appliance rental
Insurance adjusting service
Leasing service
Lecture and seminar booking service
Linen supply service
Mail order and catalog shopping service

Office supply
Package express service
Record and abstract service or title company
Roommate referral service
Tax return service
Temporary help contracting service
Travel agency
Typesetting service
Uniform supply service

Perceptual Speed, Analytical Aptitude & Associative Memory

Export/import service
Interpreting or translating service

Medical business administrative service
Medical records service

Perceptual Speed, Analytical & Diagnostic Aptitudes

Condominium management service
Convalescent home
Finance company
Fraud detection service
Gold, silver, and platinum exchange
Insurance inspection and audit service
Investment advisory service

Leasing service
Lie detection or polygraph service
Mailing list service
Paralegal training service
Real estate property management service
Secretarial training service
Travel reservations training service

Perceptual Speed & Number Memory

Auction service
Financial data information service

Inventory service
Price checking and purchasing service

Structural Visualization

Agricultural machinery distributorship
Aircraft component manufacturing
Apparel manufacturing
Boat building or manufacturing
Boring service
Building materials manufacturing
Carpet and rug manufacturing
Crane and hoist service
Dairy
Diving service
Excavating service
Fiber glass fabrication
Food processing
Foundation repair service
Furniture manufacturing
Industrial equipment distributorship
Medical equipment supply
Metals fabrication
Oil and gas production
Paving contracting
Plastics fabrication
Scientific instruments supply
Swimming pool installation and repair
  service
Textile manufacturing
Tool manufacturing
Trenching service
Water well drilling
Wrecker service for heavy trucks

Structural Visualization, Analytical and/or Diagnostic Aptitude

Accident reconstruction service
Aircraft charter, rental, and leasing service
Ambulance service
Boat charter and rental service
Body guard and physical security service
Building inspection service
Bus charter and rental service
Fire alarm system design and installation
Flight school
Industrial disposal service
Inspection and monitoring bureau
Safety analysis service

Structural Visualization & Design Memory

Box and carton design and manufacturing
Building and construction contracting
Display design, fabrication, and installation
Facilities planning and layout service
Irrigation system design and installation
Landscaping service
Outdoor advertising (billboards)
Outdoor lighting design and installation
Playground equipment design and
  manufacturing
Remodeling, renovation, and restoration
  service for buildings

Structural Visualization & Dexterities

Agricultural equipment repair and maintenance service

Air conditioning and heating installation and repair

Carpentry and cabinet making service

Construction equipment repair and maintenance service

Custom car fabrication

Gutter and downspout installation and repair

Heavy truck repair service

Machine shop

Plumbing installation and repair

Power plant repair and maintenance service

Tree service

Appendix Three

Test Your Own Aptitudes

This appendix is designed to help you evaluate *your* aptitudes. This should *not* be considered a substitute for a professionally-administered aptitude test, which requires strictly controlled testing conditions and may involve mechanical manipulations and specialized equipment. That said, if you answer the questions in this appendix thoughtfully and honestly, they *will* give you an excellent picture of *your* aptitudes...for free!

Once you identify your strong and weak aptitudes, the explanations in Chapter 2 will help you understand what they mean and how they are used in different career situations. And the charts at the end of that chapter (pp. 30—33) will show you which of the *other* chapters in this book best describe the people and business occupations that match your unique set of aptitudes.

Questionnaire

1. Do the actions and reactions of your friends and family members frequently surprise you? ❑ **YES** ❑ **NO**

2. Do/did you have trouble figuring what your teachers expect/expected from you in school? ❑ **YES** ❑ **NO**

3. Do you frequently disagree with a plan of action that everyone else in your group thinks is best? ❑ **YES** ❑ **NO**

4. Do you frequently antagonize others with your words or actions and not know about it until they tell you or you suffer repercussions from it? ❑ **YES** ❑ **NO**

5. Is it difficult for you to "put yourself in someone else's shoes?" ❑ **YES** ❑ **NO**

6. When you are working as a member of a group, do you prefer a structured approach that spells out the details of your particular job so that you do not have to worry about what the others are doing? ❑ **YES** ❑ **NO**

7. Is it difficult for you to work through others to get a job done? ❑ **YES** ❑ **NO**

8. Would you describe yourself as uncompromising and idealistic? ❑ **YES** ❑ **NO**

9. Do your family and friends tell you that you think about things differently than they do? ❑ **YES** ❑ **NO**

10. Is it easy for you to "wing it" when you meet and deal with other people? ❑ **YES** ❑ **NO**

11. Do you believe that you generally look at things the way most people do? ❑ **YES** ❑ **NO**

12. Do you understand where most other people are "coming from?" ❑ **YES** ❑ **NO**

13. Even though you may not like all of them, do you get along well with all but one or two of your coworkers? ❑ **YES** ❑ **NO**

14. Can you usually predict the actions and reactions of your friends and family? ❑ **YES** ❑ **NO**

15. Do most people see things the way you do? ❑ **YES** ❑ **NO**

16. When you are a part of a group, is it common for you to agree with the group most of the time? ❑ **YES** ❑ **NO**

17. Do you like being with a lot of people? ❑ **YES** ❑ **NO**

18. Do you think out loud? ❑ **YES** ❑ **NO**

19. Do you like a lot of hubbub? ❑ **YES** ❑ **NO**

20. Do you like to dress up so that other people will notice you? ❑ **YES** ❑ **NO**

21. Do you say what you think spontaneously? ❑ **YES** ❑ **NO**

22. Do you move at a quick pace? ❑ **YES** ❑ **NO**

23. Would other people describe you as "lively?" ❑ **YES** ❑ **NO**

24. Do you have more friends than most people? ❑ **YES** ❑ **NO**

25. At a party, do you like to circulate and talk to as many people as you can?   ❏ **YES** ❏ **NO**

26. Do you speak rather rapidly?   ❏ **YES** ❏ **NO**

27. Are you likely to start a conversation with a stranger sitting next to you in a waiting room?   ❏ **YES** ❏ **NO**

28. When you have free time, are you more likely to go shopping than for a walk by yourself?   ❏ **YES** ❏ **NO**

29. Do you procrastinate when you have projects that require you to work alone?   ❏ **YES** ❏ **NO**

30. Do you like to spend your time thinking about what has happened to you?   ❏ **YES** ❏ **NO**

31. When you have free time, are you more likely to read a book than call a friend?   ❏ **YES** ❏ **NO**

32. Do you feel drained after being at a big party for several hours?   ❏ **YES** ❏ **NO**

33. Do you usually think things out before expressing an opinion?   ❏ **YES** ❏ **NO**

34. Do you prefer not to be hurried?   ❏ **YES** ❏ **NO**

35. Are you a good listener?   ❏ **YES** ❏ **NO**

36. Do you like to reflect on ideas?   ❏ **YES** ❏ **NO**

37. Do you think that other people would describe you as "reserved?"   ❏ **YES** ❏ **NO**

38. Do you often wish that you had expressed your opinion instead of keeping quiet?   ❏ **YES** ❏ **NO**

39. Do you procrastinate when you must speak to a large group of people?   ❏ **YES** ❏ **NO**

40. When you have a disagreement with someone, do you think about it before you say anything?   ❏ **YES** ❏ **NO**

41. Do you think that people who always give other people a lot of compliments are phony?   ❏ **YES** ❏ **NO**

42. Are you "low key?"   ❏ **YES** ❏ **NO**

43. Are you irritated by people who repeat themselves many times in a conversation?   ❏ **YES** ❏ **NO**

44. Can you contribute a lot of different ideas at a brainstorming session?   ❏ **YES** ❏ **NO**

45. Do you think about unrelated ideas or events very shortly after starting a routine task?   ❏ **YES** ❏ **NO**

46. Do you have more trouble than most people when you try to concentrate on a repetitive task? ❑ **YES** ❑ **NO**

47. Do you find yourself daydreaming when you have to think about how to solve a problem? ❑ **YES** ❑ **NO**

48. Is it easy for you to explain things by using a lot of examples? ❑ **YES** ❑ **NO**

49. Do you need a lot of variety almost every day to enjoy life? ❑ **YES** ❑ **NO**

50. Are you likely to change your routine way of doing a job, just to avoid boredom? ❑ **YES** ❑ **NO**

51. Do others think that you're very imaginative? ❑ **YES** ❑ **NO**

52. Do you add a number of colorful details when you tell a story? ❑ **YES** ❑ **NO**

53. Do you wonder how you come up with the ideas you have? ❑ **YES** ❑ **NO**

54. Can you create and tell an imaginative story to a child on the spur of the moment? ❑ **YES** ❑ **NO**

55. Can you think of lots of things to say, just off the top of your head? ❑ **YES** ❑ **NO**

56. Do you have a lot of ideas, even when you don't need them? ❑ **YES** ❑ **NO**

57. Does your mind wander to a lot of different, sometimes unrelated, things when you think about how to solve a problem? ❑ **YES** ❑ **NO**

58. Is it easy for you to use a step-by-step approach for solving a problem? ❑ **YES** ❑ **NO**

59. Is it possible for you to have a messy room and still know where almost everything is? ❑ **YES** ❑ **NO**

60. Is it easy for you to make an outline or diagram? ❑ **YES** ❑ **NO**

61. Are you good at organizing your ideas? ❑ **YES** ❑ **NO**

62. Is it easy for you to make plans, even when you have many things to accomplish? ❑ **YES** ❑ **NO**

63. Is it easy for you to make analogies? ❑ **YES** ❑ **NO**

64. Do you enjoy the planning phase of a project? ❑ **YES** ❑ **NO**

65. Is it easy for you to solve a complex problem by breaking it into several simpler steps? ❑ **YES** ❑ **NO**

66. Do you take a methodical approach when you solve a problem?   ❑ YES ❑ NO

67. If a lot of limitations are placed on how you are to accomplish something, can you find a way of working within them?   ❑ YES ❑ NO

68. Do flow charts make sense to you?   ❑ YES ❑ NO

69. After hearing a description of what people in a company do and who their bosses are, could you make an organizational chart of the company?   ❑ YES ❑ NO

70. Do you automatically think of disadvantages as well as advantages when you make choices?   ❑ YES ❑ NO

71. Are you good at talking yourself out of things?   ❑ YES ❑ NO

72. Is it easy for you to solve problems by looking at clues and jumping to conclusions about what they mean?   ❑ YES ❑ NO

73. Is it natural for you to think critically about most things?   ❑ YES ❑ NO

74. Do you know the answers to most problems before you go through all the steps to solve them?   ❑ YES ❑ NO

75. Can you easily discover what's wrong with something?   ❑ YES ❑ NO

76. Is it easy for you to anticipate what an opponent will say in an argument or a debate?   ❑ YES ❑ NO

77. Can you spot pitfalls quickly?   ❑ YES ❑ NO

78. Do you take an intuitive approach when you solve a problem?   ❑ YES ❑ NO

79. Is it difficult for you to make decisions because you can see negative points as well as positive ones, no matter what you decide?   ❑ YES ❑ NO

80. Can you usually "read between the lines" and know how someone really thinks or feels, even if they don't tell you?   ❑ YES ❑ NO

81. Are you very patient and accepting when you deal with people?   ❑ YES ❑ NO

82. Do you usually have to ask when you want to find out how someone feels about something?   ❑ YES ❑ NO

83. Can you see many possibilities in a situation when most people see only a few?   ❑ YES ❑ NO

84. Is it natural for you to set goals that will take you more than five years to achieve? ❑ YES ❑ NO

85. Would you deny yourself a definite short-term reward for a long-term reward that was bigger but a little less certain? ❑ YES ❑ NO

86. Do you automatically think about your future when you make day-to-day decisions? ❑ YES ❑ NO

87. Can you live on possibilities instead of the real thing for years? ❑ YES ❑ NO

88. Do you change your long-range plans when you run into problems that make it difficult for you to carry them out? ❑ YES ❑ NO

89. Is it difficult for you to stay motivated if it will be years before you see your work pay off? ❑ YES ❑ NO

90. Did you change your college major more than twice because of a professor or course you wanted to avoid? ❑ YES ❑ NO

91. Do you need fast and frequent feedback on how you're doing to follow through on a job, especially if it's a difficult one? ❑ YES ❑ NO

92. Can you stay motivated when your efforts might not pay off for many years to come? ❑ YES ❑ NO

93. Do you need concrete, clearly defined goals to be enthusiastic about your work? ❑ YES ❑ NO

94. Will you put a lot of time and effort into a project, even though you are not sure what your reward from it will be? ❑ YES ❑ NO

95. Were (or are) you one of the first in your class to complete long multiple choice, matching, fill-in-the-blank, or true-false tests? ❑ YES ❑ NO

96. When you work with numbers, do you put your decimal point in the wrong place frequently? ❑ YES ❑ NO

97. Do you transpose numbers or letters a lot? ❑ YES ❑ NO

98. Are you likely to lose your place when you use a computer-graded answer sheet for a test? ❑ YES ❑ NO

99. Do you have trouble balancing your check book because you add or subtract incorrectly or because you record the wrong numbers? ❑ YES ❑ NO

100. If hurried, do you make more than an acceptable number of mistakes in your paperwork? ❑ **YES** ❑ **NO**

101. Do you usually get the correct answer when you add long columns of figures? ❑ **YES** ❑ **NO**

102. Do you usually have to check your paperwork and correct a lot of errors? ❑ **YES** ❑ **NO**

103. Can you fill out a form quickly without making very many mistakes? ❑ **YES** ❑ **NO**

104. When you look at the outside of a building, can you picture accurately the space inside? ❑ **YES** ❑ **NO**

105. If you see a drawing showing three sides of a five-sided object, can you easily envision the shapes of the other two sides? ❑ **YES** ❑ **NO**

106. Do you think solid geometry is easy? ❑ **YES** ❑ **NO**

107. Can you look at a contour map and easily visualize the actual terrain it represents? ❑ **YES** ❑ **NO**

108. Can you look at a diagram with pictures of unassembled parts, read the directions, and know what the finished product will look like in "real life," even though you haven't seen the actual parts? ❑ **YES** ❑ **NO**

109. Can you hear a description of a molecule and imagine what it looks like in three dimensions? ❑ **YES** ❑ **NO**

110. Can you give an accurate representation of depth or perspective when you sketch a picture? ❑ **YES** ❑ **NO**

111. Can you picture the different parts of a machine you've never seen working together if someone tells you about the machine? ❑ **YES** ❑ **NO**

112. Can you easily understand a graph that has three axes? ❑ **YES** ❑ **NO**

113. If someone described an architecturally-complicated building by telling you about its size and shape and how the different wings of the building went together, would you have a hard time picturing how the building really looked? ❑ **YES** ❑ **NO**

114. Do you have to see a machine in motion before you understand how it operates? ❑ **YES** ❑ **NO**

115. Can you visualize a three-dimensional structure in your mind without actually seeing it? ❑ **YES** ❑ **NO**

116. Can you quickly memorize foreign language vocabulary by looking at the words and their English meanings in a book? ❏ **YES** ❏ **NO**

117. Is it easy for you to learn the scientific terms for things when you know their common names? ❏ **YES** ❏ **NO**

118. Can you make high grades in a foreign language course without a lot of effort? ❏ **YES** ❏ **NO**

119. Can you remember most of the lines in a design that you see for only a few seconds? ❏ **YES** ❏ **NO**

120. When you shop, can you remember differences in the design features of the various versions of a product as you go from one store to the next? ❏ **YES** ❏ **NO**

121. Can you readily recall how a company logo looks, even if you have seen it only once or twice? ❏ **YES** ❏ **NO**

122. Do you remember most of your friends' telephone numbers? ❏ **YES** ❏ **NO**

123. Do you remember your social security, drivers license, bank account, insurance policy, and other personal identification numbers? ❏ **YES** ❏ **NO**

124. If you call information to get a phone number, do you need to write it down to remember it? ❏ **YES** ❏ **NO**

125. Are you faster than most people when you do things with your hands? ❏ **YES** ❏ **NO**

126. Are you clumsy when you have to manipulate small objects with your hands? ❏ **YES** ❏ **NO**

127. Do you drop a lot of things when you work in the kitchen? ❏ **YES** ❏ **NO**

128. Is it easy for you to use tweezers to manipulate small objects? ❏ **YES** ❏ **NO**

129. Are you quick using a needle and thread? ❏ **YES** ❏ **NO**

130. Do you have a lot of trouble getting your fingers to hit the right keys when you type? ❏ **YES** ❏ **NO**

131. Do you need to do something with your hands when you are not busy doing something else? ❏ **YES** ❏ **NO**

132. Is it easy for you to use small tools to repair delicate objects such as jewelry or electrical wires? ❏ **YES** ❏ **NO**

133. Can you sing on key? ❏ **YES** ❏ **NO**

134. Can you focus a camera precisely & quickly? ❏ **YES** ❏ **NO**

135. Can you hear small differences in pitch? ❑ **YES** ❑ **NO**

136. Can you weigh/measure things precisely? ❑ **YES** ❑ **NO**

137. Is it easy for you to do work that requires a
great deal of precision? ❑ **YES** ❑ **NO**

138. Is it easy for you to remember melodies? ❑ **YES** ❑ **NO**

139. Can you play a musical instrument by ear? ❑ **YES** ❑ **NO**

140. Is it easy for you to hear a tune and then
accurately hum it or pick it out on the piano? ❑ **YES** ❑ **NO**

141. Can you naturally keep time to music? ❑ **YES** ❑ **NO**

142. Can you easily hit a moving target? ❑ **YES** ❑ **NO**

143. Is it easy for you to catch a ball or hit a ball,
even if you have to run to put yourself in the right
place at the right time to do so? ❑ **YES** ❑ **NO**

144. Are you a good dancer? ❑ **YES** ❑ **NO**

145. Are you good at sports? ❑ **YES** ❑ **NO**

146. Can you easily remember rhythm patterns? ❑ **YES** ❑ **NO**

147. Do you have good body coordination? ❑ **YES** ❑ **NO**

148. Is it difficult for you to make your voice blend
in when you sing in a chorus? ❑ **YES** ❑ **NO**

149. When you listen to music, can you hear differ-
ences in tone quality that most people don't hear? ❑ **YES** ❑ **NO**

150. Do you have a distinctive singing voice? ❑ **YES** ❑ **NO**

151. Can you tell very small differences in the
softness and loudness of sounds? ❑ **YES** ❑ **NO**

152. When you balance the speakers on your stereo,
is it easy for you to tell which speaker is louder,
even if there is only a very small difference? ❑ **YES** ❑ **NO**

153. Are you aware of the differences in softness
and loudness when you hear classical music? ❑ **YES** ❑ **NO**

Exercise 1

On page 208 is a list of twelve "nonsense" words. Take a sheet of paper and write them down in a single column. On page 209, you will find this same list, but paired with the English "definitions" I've assigned them. Do not look at them yet! Cover page 209 before turning the page!

When you're ready to begin, use a timer or have a friend time you, and spend exactly one minute trying to memorize the English definitions of the nonsense words. When your minute is up, immediately write as many definitions as you can remember on your answer sheet. (If you copied them correctly, the nonsense words on your answer sheet will *not* be in the same order as on page 209.)

ulm	flir	oll	desu
aci	dah	onvu	scov
fef	naj	rek	toj

Exercise 2

On page 209, you will find a list of six six-digit numbers. Do not look at them yet! Use a timer or have a friend time you, and spend exactly one minute trying to memorize the numbers. Then write down as many numbers as you can remember on a separate piece of paper.

Exercise 3

This exercise is word association. When you're ready, uncover page 209, and write down in the provided space the first word you can think of when you see the word in each item.

Your word should be a spontaneous and free association, the *very first* word you can come up with. Do not go out of your way to give smart or funny answers—you will simply defeat the purpose of this exercise.

Remember to write the *first* word that comes into your mind for each word. Allow no more than 90 seconds to complete this exercise.

Exercises
(see pp. 207—208 for instructions)

Exercise 1

desu. . . .	water	flir	show	toj	rock
naj.	bird	aci	money	onvu	arm
dah.	map	rek	up	scov	shoe
fef	hard	oll	ring	ulm	friend

Exercise 2

408233	218444	900588
167189	626575	397531

Exercise 3

1. high _____
2. glass _____
3. white _____
4. work _____
5. bean _____
6. yes _____
7. picture _____
8. large _____
9. nose _____
10. sister _____
11. ring _____
12. in _____
13. card _____

14. light _____
15. south _____
16. cabinet _____
17. late _____
18. sidewalk _____
19. weak _____
20. clip _____
21. box _____
22. rug _____
23. above _____
24. note _____
25. dog _____

Scoring Guide

Here's how to score yourself on the questionnaire and exercises. As you count points, enter your totals on page 216, then use page 217 to help you summarize the results that you obtain.

Your results from the questionnaire and exercises are *not* absolute. As you read the detailed explanations of aptitudes in Chapter 2 and the rest of the chapters in the book, you may well decide to change some of the conclusions you reached on page 217.

Your Frame of Reference

Give yourself one *Specialist* point for each "Yes" answer on questions 1—9 and for each "No" answer on questions 10—16.

Give yourself one *Generalist* point for each "No" answer on questions 1—9 and for each "Yes" answer on questions 10—16.

(If you have trouble keeping track of your Specialist and Generalist answers, trying marking each with an "S" or "G" and counting how many of each you wind up with.)

The total number of possible points is 16. Turn to page 216. Write the number of Specialist points on Line 4 and the number of Generalist points on line 1.

Now turn to page 209, where you wrote your responses to the word association exercise. Give yourself one Generalist point for each answer that is the *same* as the one given below. (On a few of the items, there are two possible Generalist answers. Give yourself one Generalist point if you wrote *either one* of the words.)

Give yourself one Specialist point for each answer that is *different than* the ones shown below. Some of the words given in this exercise were "fillers," and your answers to them do not count for either Generalist or Specialist points. These answers yield no points at all and are indicated by the words "filler—0 points."

Answers to Exercise 3

1. low
2. filler—0 points
3. black
4. job or play
5. green
6. filler—0 points
7. frame
8. small
9. filler—0 points
10. filler—0 points
11. filler—0 points
12. filler—0 points

13. filler—0 points
14. dark
15. filler—0 points
16. filler—0 points
17. early
18. street or walk
19. strong

20. filler—0 points
21. filler—0 points
22. carpet
23. below or beyond
24. filler—0 points
25. cat

The total number of possible points on Exercise 3 is 13. On page 216, write the number of Specialist points from this exercise on line 5, the number of Generalist points on line 2. Then add lines 1 & 2 to get the total number of Generalist points (from the questionnaire and exercise 3 combined) and lines 4 & 5 for the total number of Specialist points.

The maximum number of total points is 29.

A score of 19 or more points in either the Specialist or the Generalist category identifies you rather definitely as one or the other.

A score of 10 or less means you probably do not fit that category.

A score between 11 and 18 points is less definite. Reading about Specialists and Generalists in Chapter 2 might help you better identify yourself. Going through questions 1 through 16 more carefully could help also.

Turn to page 217, where you can summarize your results:

If you have 19 or more Specialist points, circle "Specialist" in the Frame of Reference section.

If you have 19 or more Generalist points, circle "Generalist."

If you have between 11 and 18 points in either or both categories, circle "Uncertain."

Your Personality

Give yourself one *Extrovert* point for each "Yes" answer on questions 17—29 and for each "No" answer on questions 30—43.

Give yourself one *Introvert* point for each "No" answer on questions 17—29 and for each "Yes" answer on questions 30—43.

The total number of possible points is 27. Write your answers on lines 7 & 8 on page 216.

A score of 17 or more in either category identifies you rather clearly as an Extrovert or Introvert.

If you have 17 or more Extrovert points, circle "Extrovert" under the Personality section on page 217.

If you have 17 or more Introvert points, circle "Introvert."

If you have between 11 and 16 points, circle "Ambivert."

Your Conceptualizing Aptitudes

Ideaphoria

Give yourself one *Ideaphoria* point for each "Yes" answer on questions 44—57. The total number of possible points is 14.

If you have 11 or more points, circle "Strong Ideaphoria" on page 217; *five or fewer points,* "Weak Ideaphoria;" *6 to 10 points,* "Average Ideaphohria."

Analytical

Give yourself one Analytical point for each "Yes" answer on questions 58—69. The total number of possible points is 12.

If you have 9 or more points, circle "Strong Analytical" on page 217; *4 or fewer points,* "Weak Analytical;" *5 to 8 points,* "Average Analytical."

Diagnostic

Give yourself one Diagnostic point for each "Yes" answer on questions 70—80 and for each "No" answer on questions 81 & 82. The total number of possible points is 13.

If you have 9 or more Diagnostic points, circle "Strong Diagnostic" on page 217; *4 or fewer points,* "Weak Diagnostic;" *5 to 8 points,* "Average Diagnostic."

Your Performing Aptitudes

Foresight

Give yourself one Foresight point for each "Yes" answer on questions 83—87, 92 & 94 and for each "No" answer on questions 88—91 & 93. The total number of possible points is 12.

If you have 9 or more Foresight points, circle "Strong Foresight" on page 217; *4 or fewer points,* "Weak Foresight;" *5 to 8 points,* "Average Foresight."

Perceptual Speed

Give yourself one Perceptual Speed point for each "Yes" answer on questions 95, 101 & 103 and for each "No" answer on questions 96—100 & 102. The total number of possible points is 9.

If you have 7 or more points, circle "Strong Perceptual Speed" on page 217; *3 or fewer points,* "Weak Perceptual Speed;" *4 to 6 points,* "Average Perceptual Speed."

Structural Visualization

Give yourself one Structural Visualization point for each "Yes" answer on questions 104—112 & 115 and for each "No" answer on questions 113 & 114. The total number of possible points is 12.

If you have 9 or more points, circle "Strong Structural Visualization" on page 217; *4 or fewer points,* "Weak Structural Visualization;" *5 to 8 points,* "Average Structural Visualization."

Associative Memory

Give yourself one Associative Memory point for each "Yes" answer on questions 116—118. The total number of possible points on these questions is 3.

Now look at the paper on which you wrote your answers for Exercise 1. Give yourself one Associative Memory point for each correct answer (shown below):

ulm. . . .friend	dah. . . . . map	rek. . . . . . . up
aci. . . . money	naj. . . . . bird	desu. . . .water
fef. . . . . hard	oll. . . . . ring	scov. . . . . shoe
flir. . . . . show	onvu. . . . arm	toj. . . . . . rock

The total number of possible points for Exercise 1 is 12.

Now add the number of Associative Memory points you got on questions 116 through 118 to the points you got on Exercise 1. The maximum number of possible points is 15.

If you scored 11 or more points, circle "Strong Associative Memory" on page 217; *5 or fewer points,* "Weak Associative Memory;" *6 to 10 points,* "Average Associative Memory."

Design Memory

Give yourself one Design Memory point for each "Yes" answer on questions 119—121. The total number of possible points on these questions is 3.

If you have 3 points, circle "Strong Design Memory" on page 217; *0 or 1 point,* "Weak Design Memory;" *2 points,* "Average Design Memory."

Number Memory

Give yourself one Number Memory point for each "Yes" answer on questions 122—124. The total number of possible points on these questions is 3.

Now compare the numbers you wrote down with the numbers you tried to memorize on page 209.

Give yourself two Number Memory points for each *entire* six-digit number you correctly remembered.

Give yourself one Number Memory point if you got three *consecutive* digits within a number right but did not remember the entire number. The total number of possible points for Exercise 2 is 12.

Now add the Number Memory points you have from questions 122 through 124 to the points you have on Exercise 2. The maximum number of possible points is 15.

If you have 11 or more Number Memory points, circle "Strong Number Memory" on page 217; *6 or fewer* points, "Weak Number Memory;" *7 to 10 points,* "Average Number Memory."

Finger Dexterity

Give yourself one Finger Dexterity point for a "Yes" answer on question 125 and for each "No" answer on questions 126 & 127. The total number of possible points on these questions is 3.

If you have 3 points, circle "Strong Finger Dexterity" on page 217; *0 or 1 point,* "Weak Finger Dexterity;" *2 points,* "Average Finger Dexterity."

Instrument Dexterity

Give yourself one Instrument Dexterity point for each "Yes" answer on questions 128, 129, 131 & 132 and for a "No" answer to question 130. The total number of possible points is 5.

If you have 4 or 5 points, circle "Strong Instrument Dexterity" on page 217; *0 or 1 point,* "Weak Instrument Dexterity;" *2 or 3 points,* "Average Instrument Dexterity."

Pitch Discrimination

Give yourself one Pitch Discrimination point for each "Yes" answer on questions 133—137. The total number of possible points on these questions is 5.

If you have 4 or 5 points, circle "Strong Pitch Discrimination" on page 217; *0 or 1 point,* "Weak Pitch Discrimination;" *2 or 3 points,* "Average Pitch Discrimination."

Tonal Memory

Give yourself one Tonal Memory point for each "Yes" answer on questions 138—140. The total number of possible points on these questions is 3.

If you have 2 or 3 points, circle "Strong Tonal Memory" on page 217; *0 points,* "Weak Tonal Memory;" *1 point,* "Average Tonal Memory."

Time Discrimination

Give yourself one Time Discrimination point for each "Yes" answer on questions 141—145. The total number of possible points on these questions is 5.

If you have 4 or 5 points, circle "Strong Time Discrimination" on page 217; *0 points,* "Weak Time Discrimination;" *1—3 points,* "Average Time Discrimination."

Rhythm Memory

Give yourself one Rhythm Memory point for each "Yes" answer on questions 144—147. (Questions 144 and 145 are counted for both Rhythm Memory and Time Discrimination.) The total number of possible points on these questions is 4.

If you have 3 or 4 points, circle "Strong Rhythm Memory" on page 217; *0 or 1 point,* "Weak Rhythm Memory;" *2 points,* circle "Average Rhythm Memory."

Timbre Discrimination

Give yourself one Timbre Discrimination point for each "Yes" answer on questions 148—150. The total number of possible points is 3.

If you have 3 points, circle "Strong Timbre Discrimination" on page 217; *0 points,* "Weak Timbre Discrimination;" *1 or 2 points,* "Average Timbre Discrimination."

Loudness Discrimination

Give yourself one Loudness Discrimination point for each "Yes" answer on questions 151—153. The total number of possible points is 3.

If you have 3 points, circle "Strong Loudness Discrimination" on page 217; *0 points,* "Weak Loudness Discrimination;" *1 or 2 points,* "Average Loudness Discrimination."

Scoring Summary

Line 1: Generalist points from Questionnaire   _____

Line 2: Generalist points from Exercise 3   _____

Line 3: Total Generalist points (Lines 1 + 2)   _____

Line 4: Specialist points from Questionnaire   _____

Line 5: Specialist points from Exercise 3   _____

Line 6: Total Specialist points (Lines 1 + 2)   _____

Line 7: Total Extrovert Points   _____

Line 8: Total Introvert Points   _____

Your Aptitude Summary

FRAME OF REFERENCE

Specialist	Generalist	Uncertain

PERSONALITY

Extrovert	Introvert	Ambivert

CONCEPTUALIZING APTITUDES

Ideaphoria	Strong	Average	Weak
Analytical	Strong	Average	Weak
Diagnostic	Strong	Average	Weak

PERFORMING APTITUDES

Foresight	Strong	Average	Weak
Perceptual Speed	Strong	Average	Weak
Structural Visualization	Strong	Average	Weak
Associative Memory	Strong	Average	Weak
Design Memory	Strong	Average	Weak
Number Memory	Strong	Average	Weak
Finger Dexterity	Strong	Average	Weak
Instrument Dexterity	Strong	Average	Weak
Pitch Discrimination	Strong	Average	Weak
Tonal Memory	Strong	Average	Weak
Time Discrimination	Strong	Average	Weak
Rhythm Memory	Strong	Average	Weak
Timbre Discrimination	Strong	Average	Weak
Loudness Discrimination	Strong	Average	Weak

Index

❏ **Your First Resume: The Essential Comprehensive Guide for Anyone Entering or Reentering the Job Market (2nd Edition)** by Ronald W. Fry. Paper, 8 1/2 x 11, 192 pp., $10.95

❏ **Work in the New Economy: Careers and Job Seeking into the 21st Century,** by Robert Wegmann, Robert Chapman and Miriam Johnson, Paper, 6 x 9, 303 pp., $14.95.

❏ **The Complete Guide to International Jobs & Careers** by Drs. Ron & Caryl Krannich, Paper, 6 x 9, 236 pp., $13.95

❏ **Your First Book of Wealth** by A. David Silver ISBN 0-934829-47-0, Paper, 6 x 9, 224 pp., $10.95.

❏ **High Impact Resumes and Letters,** 4th Edition, by Krannich and Banis, Paper, 7 x 10, 180 pp., $12.95

❏ **Interview for Success,** by Drs. Caryl & Ron Krannich. Paper, 6 x 9, 176 pp., $11.95

❏ **The Complete Guide to Public Employment,** by Drs. Ron and Caryl Krannich, Paper, 6 x 9, 483 pp., $15.95.

❏ **Careering & Recareering for the 1990s** by Ronald L. Krannich Paper, 6 x 9, 192 pp., $12.95

❏ **Network Your Way to Job and Career Success** by Drs. Ron & Caryl Krannich, Paper, 6 x 9, 180 pp., $11.95

TO ORDER ANY TITLES OR REQUEST A CATALOG:

CALL 1-800-CAREER-1
TO USE YOUR MASTERCARD OR VISA.

Or send price as indicated, plus appropriate shipping and handling (please enclose $2.50 per order and $1.00 per title for each book ordered) to:

The Career Press
62 Beverly Rd., PO Box 34
Hawthorne, NJ 07507